*Test Yourself in*

# EVIDENCE
# CIVIL PROCEDURE
# CRIMINAL PROCEDURE
# SENTENCING

*Test Yourself in*

# EVIDENCE
# CIVIL PROCEDURE
# CRIMINAL PROCEDURE
# SENTENCING

Inns of Court
School of Law

BLACKSTONE
PRESS LIMITED

First published in Great Britain 1994 by Blackstone Press Limited,
9–15 Aldine Street, London W12 8AW. Telephone 081-740 1173

© The Council of Legal Education, 1994

ISBN: 1 85431 389 4

British Library Cataloguing in Publication Data
A CIP catalogue record for this book is available from the British
Library.

Typeset by Style Photosetting Limited, Mayfield, East Sussex
Printed by W M Print Limited, Walsall, West Midlands

# CONTENTS

# FOREWORD

This book has been published in conjunction with the Inns of Court School of Law, which runs the Bar Vocational Course. The course, which was introduced in 1989, was specifically designed to equip students with the evidential and procedural knowledge and the practical skills they will need to start their professional careers. It is gratifying to find that the course has been greeted as a major step forward in legal vocational training, and that it has attracted so much interest, both at home and overseas.

This book has been prepared by senior teaching staff at the Inns of Court School of Law and its primary purpose is to meet the needs of students enrolled on the Bar Vocational Course for 'mock' Multiple Choice Tests (MCTs) in order to test themselves in the important subjects of Evidence, Civil Litigation, Criminal Litigation and Sentencing prior to the MCTs in these subjects conducted annually at the School. The MCTs are designed to test whether students have the sound working knowledge and comprehension of these subjects that they will need in pupillage and the early years of practice. Although produced for a specific course, the book should also be of enormous interest and use to all students who wish to test themselves in these subjects, and their tutors.

This publication will be revised annually, to keep it up to date and to improve its content with the benefit of experience and comments made by its readers. Comments are always welcome and may be addressed either to the Dean or the Course Director at the Inns of Court School of Law.

The continuing enthusiasm of the staff of Blackstone Press Ltd and their efficiency in arranging the production and publication of this book is much appreciated.

*The Hon. Mr Justice Phillips*
*Chairman of the Council of Legal Education*
*December 1994*

# INTRODUCTION

**PLEASE DO NOT ATTEMPT, OR EVEN READ,
THE MULTIPLE CHOICE TEST QUESTIONS
CONTAINED IN THIS BOOK UNTIL YOU HAVE READ
THIS INTRODUCTION!**

## A.  THE PURPOSE OF THE MULTIPLE CHOICE TESTS

It must be rare, on opening a book and turning to its first page, to be greeted by a command, albeit a polite command. However, there is a very good reason for such a command: that if you do embark upon testing yourself before you have read the following few pages on (a) the purpose of the Multiple Choice Tests (MCTs) (b) the nature and format of the MCTs (c) popular misconceptions and (d) advice on taking the tests, then it is likely that you will simply defeat the purposes of the MCTs.

The MCTs contained in this book have two purposes. The first is to enable you to test, with speed and accuracy, whether you have a sound working knowledge and comprehension of the main principles of law and procedure, and the leading cases, in Evidence, Civil Litigation, Criminal Litigation and Sentencing. The MCT questions used are directed at the general rules, the principal exceptions to those rules and the leading authorities. Wherever possible, they concentrate on the modern law and important decisions. They are not directed at narrow, antiquated, abstruse or esoteric points that a practitioner, or even a scholar, might properly need to look up and research. This explains why, as we shall see, each question has to be answered in only $2\frac{1}{2}$ minutes or less.

The second purpose is to enable you, after the test, to identify, with precision, your weaknesses, the gaps in your knowledge and understanding, so that you can revisit these areas and take appropriate remedial action.

## B. THE NATURE AND FORMAT OF THE MCTs

This book contains two MCTs which, in terms of style and difficulty, closely resemble the two-stage MCTs conducted annually on the Bar Vocational Course.

*MCT – Part 1*

The first MCT, which is called MCT – Part 1, comprises 60 questions, to be taken at one sitting, and incorporates questions on only *some* subjects normally found in the syllabus for courses in Evidence, Civil Procedure and Criminal Procedure. The subjects in question are set out in Appendix 5. Therefore you should not attempt MCT – Part 1 until you have completed your studies in all of the subjects in question.

The 60 questions of MCT – Part 1 have to be answered in no more than 2½ hours. This means that if you divide the time equally between the questions, you will have 2 minutes and 30 seconds to answer each question.

*MCT – Part 2*

The second MCT, MCT – Part 2, is more demanding than MCT – Part 1, because it contains more questions, covers more syllabus subjects, and gives you less time to answer each question. MCT – Part 2 comprises 80 questions, to be taken at one sitting, and incorporates questions on *all* subjects normally found on the syllabus for courses in Evidence, Civil Procedure, Criminal Procedure and Sentencing. The subjects in question are set out in Appendix 6. Therefore you should not attempt MCT – Part 2 until you have completed your studies in all of the subjects in question.

The 80 questions of MCT – Part 2 have to be answered in 3 hours. This means that if you divide the time equally between the questions, you will have 2 minutes and 15 seconds to answer each question.

Both MCTs use the following headings to identify the subject matter of the various questions: CIVIL LITIGATION, CIVIL EVIDENCE, CRIMINAL LITIGATION (or CRIMINAL LITIGATION AND SENTENCING) and CRIMINAL EVIDENCE. So, if you wish to complete only part or parts of the MCTS, e.g. the Civil Evidence questions only, you should recalculate the length of the test by reference to the number of questions you intend to attempt.

*Format*

The questions in the MCTs contained in this book are always accompanied by four possible answers: [A], [B], [C] and [D]. You are required to select just one answer, the one that you think is correct/the best. You should record the answers you select on a separate question sheet (detachable from the inside back cover of this book), by putting a pencil line through [A], [B], [C] or [D]. (Pencils allow you to change your mind and use an eraser!)

The questions often often take the form of a factual problem and conclude with a specific question, such as 'On these facts, what is the most appropriate advice to give to the client?' or 'On these facts, which of the following orders is the judge most likely to make?'. Questions of this kind are designed to test whether you are able to recognise the law or procedure appropriate to the given facts and/or whether you are able to apply the law to the facts and thereby identify the correct outcome.

Other questions take the form of a number of legal propositions, only one of which is correct or, as the case may be, incorrect, or ask about a specific point of law. Thus as to the former, the question may read, 'Which of the following propositions is correct?' or 'Which of the following propositions is INCORRECT?'. As to the latter, the question may state a rule of law and then conclude, for example, 'Which of the following is NOT an exception to this general rule?'. Questions of this kind are designed to test your knowledge of the law.

Some questions combine both a factual scenario and a choice of legal propositions so that, after setting out the facts, the question may read, for example, 'Which of the following best describes the principles which the Court should apply to these facts?'.

Most of the questions contained in the MCTs in this book were originally created for, and have been used on, the Bar Vocational Course. A lot of effort properly goes into the creation and validation of such questions. Every question devised for use at the Inns of Court School of Law is thoroughly scrutinised by (i) senior members of staff specialising in the subject in question (ii) specialist practitioners and (iii) the members of the Board of Examiners, who include academics, practitioners and judges with a broad range of experience and expertise. Every effort is made to ensure that each question is clear, unambiguous and fair, with only one correct answer and three incorrect answers.

After each MCT, the results are then subjected to an item-by-item statistical analysis, to show the facility, selectivity and reliability of each question. Facility simply means the proportion of candidates who answered the question correctly – it indicates how easy or difficult that particular question was. Selectivity is a measure of the correlation between those who answer a particular question correctly and those who do well in the test overall. A high selectivity rating shows that most 'good' candidates have answered the question correctly. Reliability is a measure of the overall effectiveness of the question, the product of facility and selectivity. If there is an average facility and a high selectivity, the question is very reliable at differentiating between 'good' and 'bad' candidates.

Using this statistical information, it is possible to review, and if necessary amend, questions. For example, it may be desirable to amend or delete a question with an unduly high or low facility rating. Equally, in the case of a question with an unduly low selectivity or reliability rating, it is important to revisit the question to see whether it contained some ambiguity or was otherwise misleading, which might explain why 'good' candidates were getting it wrong.

## C. MCTs — POPULAR MISCONCEPTIONS

*'MCTs are easier than traditional examinations'*

This view tends to be expressed by those who have never sat an MCT. By contrast, the experience of students who have taken MCTs, both at home and overseas, is that such tests are much more demanding than traditional examinations. There are three principal reasons for this.

First, MCTs allow examiners to cover the whole syllabus. For students who have been brought up on conventional examinations and who have adopted the 'question-spotting' approach, the MCT obviously comes as a very nasty shock!

Secondly, the MCT offers no scope for the candidate who would waffle. In conventional examinations, some students, unaware or not too sure of the correct answers, will hedge their bets, setting out at length all such seemingly relevant legal knowledge as they possess, but making no real effort to apply the law, simply skirting around the central issues with deliberate equivocation. There is no scope for such tactics in the MCT: faced with 4 competing answers, only one of which is correct, you must nail your colours to the mast.

Thirdly, there is the obvious pressure that comes from having to answer some 60 (or 80) questions at the rate of $2\frac{1}{2}$ (or $2\frac{1}{4}$) minutes per question. This calls for the ability to analyse, digest and comprehend material at speed, before reaching a firm conclusion, only to move on to repeat the exercise in the next question, and so on.

*'MCT means multiple guess or passing by good luck'*

It is perfectly accurate to say that if you go into the examination room with no relevant knowledge at all and sit an MCT in which each question has four competing answers, then by the law of averages you *could* score 25%. However, the pass-mark is usually more than double 25%. On the Bar Vocational Course, for example, a student who answers correctly 60% of all the questions set, will achieve a bare pass; and in many jurisdictions the percentage required to pass is much higher. Students relying on guesswork or Lady Luck simply do not pass. However, as will be stressed below, when you do not know, or are unsure about, the correct answer to a particular question, you *should* make an intelligent guess, because no mark is deducted for a wrong answer.

*'MCTs are inferior to traditional tests and examinations'*

The validity of this criticism depends upon what one is seeking to test or examine. Obviously the MCT is not an appropriate tool to test oral legal skills such as Advocacy or Negotiation, just as it would be an inappropriate means of testing the practical skills of a pianist or an airline pilot. Equally, it cannot test a student's *written* skills, whether in drafting a pleading, writing a legal essay or answering a legal problem (although it is interesting to note, in passing, that there is a high degree of correlation between student results in MCTs and in other forms of testing which do involve oral performances and written work). However, experience shows that the MCT is an excellent vehicle for testing, with accuracy, reading ability, powers of analysis, and levels of knowledge and comprehension. MCTs have been used to test doctors at both undergraduate and postgraduate level, and in other disciplines, for many years. Moreover, there is no question of examiner bias.

*'MCTs cannot test the "grey areas"'*

This is simply incorrect! For every 'grey area' question, there can be a suitably 'grey area' answer. For example, if on a particular point the authorities conflict, the correct answer may simply read, 'The authorities are in conflict on this point'. (Note, however, that such wording may also be used for an incorrect answer, i.e. in a question where the authorities are not in conflict at all.) Another possibility, in 'grey areas', is to build a question around the facts of an important reported case, thereby testing whether a student knows of, and has understood, that case. That said, it is certainly true that it can be more demanding to set good MCT questions on 'grey areas', and for this reason they tend to be avoided, unless they concern important areas of the law.

## D.   ADVICE ON TAKING THE TESTS

The purpose of the MCTs in this book is likely to be defeated unless you observe certain basic rules.

*1. DO NOT ATTEMPT AN MCT UNTIL YOU HAVE COMPLETED YOUR STUDIES IN THE SUBJECTS COVERED*

The MCTs in this book are designed to be taken only *after* you have completed your studies in the subject areas covered and *before* you are formally examined in them.

*2. TAKE THE MCT UNDER EXAMINATION CONDITIONS*

Make sure that you will have an *uninterrupted* period of $2\frac{1}{2}$ or, as appropriate, 3 hours, in which to complete the *whole test*. (If you wish to complete only part or parts of either MCT, for example the Evidence questions only, you should recalculate the length of the test by reference to the number of questions you intend to attempt and the number of permitted minutes per question: $2\frac{1}{2}$ minutes for Part 1, $2\frac{1}{4}$ minutes for Part 2.) If you are working at home, tell the other residents that you do not wish to be disturbed, and take the telephone off the hook! Also remove from the room any relevant books or materials that you might be tempted to use – the MCT is a closed-book examination.

*3. USE THE ANSWER SHEET*

On starting the test, detach the appropriate Answer Sheet from the inside back cover of this book and read carefully the Instructions on that Answer Sheet.

*4. OBSERVE THE TIME LIMITS*

Observe the overall time limit of $2\frac{1}{2}$ or 3 hours (if necessary by using an alarm clock) and try to spend no longer than an average of $2\frac{1}{2}$ minutes (Part 1) or $2\frac{1}{4}$ minutes (Part 2) on each question. You will doubtless find that some of the questions can be answered in less time, whereas others require slightly more time – the questions vary in length and difficulty. However, the overall time limit reflects the standard of the MCT as a whole, and should not be exceeded.

*5. READ ALL FOUR COMPETING ANSWERS TO EACH QUESTION BEFORE MAKING A SELECTION*

Whether a problem-type question or a propositions-type question, you should *always* look at all four competing answers before making a selection. There are three good reasons for doing so.

First, an answer may refer to another answer or answers. For example, the question may set out a judge's ruling on a particular point of law, and conclude, 'Which of the following reasons could justify the judge's ruling?'. [A] may then set out one reason and suggest that this *alone* could justify the ruling; [B] may set out a different reason and suggest that this *alone* could justify the ruling; and [C] may read, 'The reasons in both [A] and [B]'.

Secondly, even when you are relatively confident that you know the correct answer before you even look at the options on offer, and you are therefore tempted to simply select the 'correct' answer and to ignore the other answers, reading those other answers to check that they are indeed incorrect is the best way of confirming your initial selection.

Thirdly, there may well be occasions when you are unsure as to the correct answer. In these circumstances, it is often possible to identify the correct answer by the process of eliminating others which you know to be incorrect. Often you will find that the question-setter has included one answer which is quite obviously incorrect and another which is also incorrect, although not quite so obviously, thereby reducing the effective choice from four to two – the two remaining answers will test whether you have understood the legal principle in question.

## 6.   TREAT THE EXAMINERS AS IF INFALLIBLE

If your initial reaction, on reading a particular question and the four competing answers, is that you need more factual information before you can select the correct answer, or that there are two correct answers, or that the correct answer seems to have been omitted, quickly swallow your pride and re-read the question to see if there is something which you have missed or the importance of which you failed to take note on the first reading. If, having re-read the question and answers, you remain convinced that you need more information, or that there are two correct answers, or no correct answer, then select the answer which, in your opinion, gets nearest to being correct or is the best from which you have to make a choice. Remember that most of the questions have been thoroughly scrutinised by specialist academics and practitioners and statistically tested in terms of their selectivity and reliability (see above).

## 7.  IF NECESSARY, MAKE AN INTELLIGENT GUESS

As already explained, multiple choice does not mean multiple guess or passing by good luck. However, if having read a particular question, you do not know the correct answer and are unable to eliminate all of the incorrect answers, then you *should* make an intelligent guess, and move on. As we shall see, you do *not* lose a mark for a wrong answer.

## 8.  MARK YOUR PERFORMANCE

After you have completed the MCT – and probably after a break of suitable length – you will want to mark your performance. You will find the correct answers to MCT – Part 1 and MCT – Part 2 listed in Appendix 1 and Appendix 2 respectively. Award yourself one mark for each question that you have answered correctly. If you have selected one of the other three answers to the question, you should *not* subtract a mark – you simply gain no mark for that question. You may then rate your overall performance according to the following table.

|  | MCT – Part 1 | MCT – Part 2 | Comment |
|---|---|---|---|
| Number of questions answered correctly | 0–35 | 0–47 | A performance ranging from the awful to the weak. At best, on 35, you are showing insufficient knowledge and comprehension in over 40% of all subjects tested. |
|  | 36–44 | 48–59 | A performance ranging from one of bare competence to competence. You are showing insufficient knowledge and comprehension in 26–40% of all subjects tested. |
|  | 48–53 | 60–71 | A performance ranging from the competent to the very competent. You are showing insufficient knowledge and comprehension in 11–25% of all subjects tested. |
|  | 54–60 | 72–80 | A performance ranging from the very competent to the outstanding. You are showing insufficient knowledge and comprehension in only 10% or less of all subjects tested. |

## 9. REVIEW YOUR PERFORMANCE

After you have marked your performance, take a break! You need to be fully refreshed before you embark upon the most important part of the exercise, namely the review of your performance by reference to the note-form answers to the questions of MCT – Part 1 and MCT – Part 2, which you will find in Appendix 3 and Appendix 4 respectively. Thorough review is important because it allows you to identify with precision the gaps in your knowledge and understanding of the law with a view to further work or revision.

Look at *all* of the note-form answers, not just those to the questions which you got wrong. By looking at the answers to the questions which you answered correctly, you will usually confirm your understanding of the law. Sometimes, however, you may discover that although your answer was in fact correct, your reasoning was defective. Equally, you need to know the reasons for the answers as to which you could only make an inspired guess.

# MCT – Part 1

# [TIME LIMIT: 2½ HOURS]

## CIVIL LITIGATION

**1.** Mavis, who is retired, is suing a bus company for damages in respect of an injury to her leg. She suffered a double fracture of her left femur (thigh bone). She spent 2 days in hospital, but was treated mainly in the Outpatients Department. Her final cast was removed 8 months after the injury was sustained. The medical evidence indicates there is no permanent disability and no risk of future osteoarthritis.

Mavis further claims £120 for damage to her clothing, but has lost no income. Which one of the following correctly describes where proceedings should be commenced?

[A] A County Court, because this is a personal injuries claim.

[B] A County Court, because this is a personal injuries claim with a value almost certainly below £50,000.

[C] The High Court, because this is an action in tort.

[D] The High Court, because this is an action for unliquidated damages.

**2.** The Court of Appeal in *Anton Piller KG* v *Manufacturing Processes Ltd* (1976) laid down a number of pre-conditions for the making of an *Anton Piller* order. Three of the four following propositions accurately reflect conditions stated by the Court of Appeal. One does not. Which one?

[A] There must be clear evidence that the defendants have in their possession incriminating documents or things, and that there is a real possibility that they may destroy such material before any application inter partes can be made.

[B] The damage, actual or potential, must be very serious for the plaintiff.

[C] The action must concern the infringement of intellectual property rights.

[D] The plaintiff must show an extremely strong prima facie case on the merits.

**3.** Julia has issued a generally indorsed writ in the High Court against Rick alleging breach of contract. The only remedy she seeks is specific performance of the contract. More than a month has passed since the date of service and Rick has not acknowledged service. Julia wants advice about entering judgment in default under RSC Ord. 13 at this stage. Which one of the following propositions is correct?

[A] Judgment in default of notice of intention to defend is not possible because Julia's claim is for equitable relief which falls outside the scope of RSC Ord. 13.

[B] Judgment in default is not possible because Julia's claim for specific performance should have been commenced by originating summons, to which the default procedure does not apply.

[C] Judgment in default can be entered because the time for acknowledging service has expired, and no notice of intention to defend has been given.

[D] Judgment in default of notice of intention to defend might be obtained, but only with the leave of the Court.

4.   Eric builds a house for Kate. The house is defective. Kate sues Eric in the High Court. Eric says that the fault was due to bad workmanship by George, one of his sub-contractors. Eric also claims that George damaged some of his equipment. Eric issues a third party notice against George claiming an indemnity in respect of any damages awarded against him together with damages for the damaged equipment. Kate's action against Eric is dismissed for want of prosecution. Which one of the following statements is correct?

[A]   Both of Eric's claims against George fall with Kate's claim against Eric, and so Eric will have to issue a writ against George.

[B]   Both of Eric's claims against George continue together as an independent action.

[C]   Eric's claim for an indemnity falls with Kate's claim, but his claim for damages continues as an independent action.

[D]   Both of Eric's claims against George continue, but the Court will order separate trials because the relief claimed is not of the same or a similar nature.

**5.** Marine Fish Ltd, a large trawler concern operating around Dover, has suffered severe losses due, it says, to the dumping of phosphates off the French coast by the large French soap powder producers, Savon Inc. Assume that there is a good cause of action against the defendant, that the tort was committed in France and that Marine Fish Ltd suffered damage in England. Marine Fish Ltd wishes to know whether it can pursue a claim against Savon Inc. within the jurisdiction.

Which one of the following statements is *correct*?

[A] Since Savon Inc. is domiciled in France, a contracting state to the Brussels Convention, the claim must be pursued in France.

[B] Since the tort was committed on French territory, the claim must be pursued in France.

[C] Since the damage was sustained in England, Marine Fish Ltd should seek leave to serve the writ out of the jurisdiction under RSC Ord. 11.

[D] Since the damage was sustained in England, Marine Fish Ltd can sue Savon Inc. in France or in England. The choice is with Marine Fish Ltd. If it chooses to sue within the jurisdiction no leave is required to serve the writ.

**6.** You are instructed on behalf of Howard, who has been served with a writ and an ex parte injunction restraining him from publishing an allegedly defamatory article about Agnes.

Howard has sworn an affidavit asserting that the contents of the draft article are true, and has applied to discharge the injunction. Which one of the following propositions best describes the principle that will be applied on the application?

[A] Provided there is a serious issue on the question of defamation, the Court will consider the adequacy of damages to either side and the balance of convenience.

[B] As Howard has stated on affidavit that he intends to plead justification, the injunction should ordinarily be discharged to protect freedom of speech unless the alleged libel is obviously untrue.

[C] As Howard has stated on affidavit that he intends to plead justification, the injunction will be discharged to protect freedom of speech, and the Court will not investigate the veracity of Howard's affidavit.

[D] As the application is likely finally to dispose of the dispute, the injunction will be continued only if the merits of Agnes's case are overwhelming.

**7.** Robert moored his yacht 'Swift' alongside a quay at 7.30 am in a small North Wales village. When he reached the top of the steps he noticed an artist painting the harbour. He then set out for the nearby town with Miles, his crewman, for stores. On their return at 11 am they were aghast to find the 'Swift' severely damaged after a collision. There were several fairly large fishing vessels in the harbour. The artist was still painting. When Robert asked if he had seen what happened, the artist said that it was against his principles to tell tales on anyone. At the post office Robert found out that the artist was Vincent Morgan, and that he lived in the village. No one else seems to have seen anything. You are instructed to advise Robert.

Which one of the following is the most appropriate advice to give him?

[A] That an originating summons be issued against Vincent requesting pre-action discovery pursuant to the Supreme Court Act 1981, s. 33(2).

[B] That a writ be issued claiming a *Norwich Pharmacal* order against Vincent.

[C] That no pre-action discovery is available against Vincent ecause he is protected by the privilege against self-incrimination.

[D] That no pre-action discovery is available against Vincent because he is a mere witness.

**8.** David, a tenant, made out a cheque for £6,000 in favour of Peter, his landlord, in respect of rent due. On presentation, the cheque was dishonoured and accordingly Peter issued a summons against David with Particulars of Claim claiming £6,000 due on the cheque. David has filed a defence and counterclaimed for damages of £4,000 for breach by Peter of a covenant in the lease to carry out certain repairs to the rented property (which has diminished the rental value of the property). Peter has now applied for summary judgment under CCR Ord. 9, r. 14.

Which one of the following orders is the District Judge most likely to make?

[A]  Unconditional leave to defend.

[B]  Judgment for the plaintiff in the sum of £6,000.

[C]  Judgment for the plaintiff in the sum of £2,000 with unconditional leave to defend as to the remainder of the plaintiff's claim (i.e. £4,000).

[D]  Judgment for the plaintiff in the sum of £6,000 but with a stay of execution in respect of £4,000 of the said £6,000 pending the trial of the counterclaim.

158

1 [A] [B] [C] [D]
2 [A] [B] [C] [D]
3 [A] [B] [C] [D]
4 [A] [B] [C] [D]
5 [A] [B] [C] [D]
6 [A] [B] [C] [D]
7 [A] [B] [C] [D]
8 [A] [B] [C] [D]
9 [A] [B] [C] [D]
10 [A] [B] [C] [D]
11 [A] [B] [C] [D]
12 [A] [B] [C] [D]
13 [A] [B] [C] [D]
14 [A] [B] [C] [D]
15 [A] [B] [C] [D]
16 [A] [B] [C] [D]
17 [A] [B] [C] [D]
18 [A] [B] [C] [D]
19 [A] [B] [C] [D]
20 [A] [B] [C] [D]
21 [A] [B] [C] [D]
22 [A] [B] [C] [D]
23 [A] [B] [C] [D]
24 [A] [B] [C] [D]
25 [A] [B] [C] [D]
26 [A] [B] [C] [D]
27 [A] [B] [C] [D]
28 [A] [B] [C] [D]
29 [A] [B] [C] [D]
30 [A] [B] [C] [D]
31 [A] [B] [C] [D]
32 [A] [B] [C] [D]
33 [A] [B] [C] [D]
34 [A] [B] [C] [D]
35 [A] [B] [C] [D]
36 [A] [B] [C] [D]
37 [A] [B] [C] [D]
38 [A] [B] [C] [D]
39 [A] [B] [C] [D]
40 [A] [B] [C] [D]
41 [A] [B] [C] [D]
42 [A] [B] [C] [D]
43 [A] [B] [C] [D]
44 [A] [B] [C] [D]
45 [A] [B] [C] [D]
46 [A] [B] [C] [D]
47 [A] [B] [C] [D]
48 [A] [B] [C] [D]
49 [A] [B] [C] [D]
50 [A] [B] [C] [D]
51 [A] [B] [C] [D]
52 [A] [B] [C] [D]
53 [A] [B] [C] [D]
54 [A] [B] [C] [D]
55 [A] [B] [C] [D]
56 [A] [B] [C] [D]
57 [A] [B] [C] [D]
58 [A] [B] [C] [D]
59 [A] [B] [C] [D]
60 [A] [B] [C] [D]
61 [A] [B] [C] [D]
62 [A] [B] [C] [D]
63 [A] [B] [C] [D]
64 [A] [B] [C] [D]
65 [A] [B] [C] [D]
66 [A] [B] [C] [D]
67 [A] [B] [C] [D]
68 [A] [B] [C] [D]
69 [A] [B] [C] [D]
70 [A] [B] [C] [D]
71 [A] [B] [C] [D]
72 [A] [B] [C] [D]
73 [A] [B] [C] [D]
74 [A] [B] [C] [D]
75 [A] [B] [C] [D]
76 [A] [B] [C] [D]
77 [A] [B] [C] [D]
78 [A] [B] [C] [D]
79 [A] [B] [C] [D]
80 [A] [B] [C] [D]

# ANSWER SHEET

Read the instructions before you start to fill in the answers.

## INSTRUCTIONS

1. Use the HB pencil provided.
2. Fill in the boxes like this ▬ not like this ⬦ ✗ ✓
3. Fill in the boxes to indicate the subjects and whether this is a resit.
4. Write in your candidate number and the examination date in the spaces provided **and** fill in the boxes below.
5. Write your name and signature in the spaces provided.
6. Each question has four possible answers lettered A to D. Read all four answers **in full** before making a selection. Select the answer which you think is correct/best and indicate it on the answer sheet by filling in the appropriate box.
7. If you fill in 2 or more boxes in any question, that question will carry no mark.
8. Erase all mistakes thoroughly using the eraser provided.

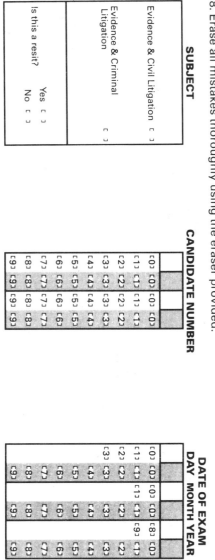

## SUBJECT

Evidence & Civil Litigation [ ]

Evidence & Criminal Litigation [ ]

Is this a resit?

Yes [ ]
No [ ]

## CANDIDATE NUMBER

## DATE OF EXAM
### DAY MONTH YEAR

**9.** Isaac is claiming damages from his employer, Highbury Upholstery Ltd, in respect of a respiratory disease he alleges he contracted from involuntary inhalation of products used in the factory where he works. Eighteen months ago Isaac made an application to the Department of Social Security (DSS) for industrial disablement benefit. This involved completing an application form and attending a medical board, which completed a written report form. Highbury intend to apply for disclosure of these documents from the DSS.

Which one of the following propositions is correct?

[A] Highbury can only obtain an order for disclosure against the DSS after proceedings are commenced, the application being made by interlocutory summons.

[B] Highbury can only obtain an order for disclosure against the DSS after proceedings are commenced, the application being made by originating summons.

[C] Highbury can first obtain an order for disclosure against the DSS before action, the application being made by originating summons.

[D] Highbury cannot obtain an order against the DSS for disclosure (other than by subpoena) because Isaac's claim is not for personal injuries.

**10.** Mark is injured in an accident at his place of work. He alleges that the machine in question was badly maintained and he believes that there have been similar accidents before. He brings County Court proceedings against his employer. In discovery by lists, no mention is made in the employer's list of documents of accident reports relating to the earlier accidents involving the machinery. In these circumstances Mark may do any of the following things except one. Which one?

[A] Apply for an order compelling the employer to attend before the District Judge for cross-examination as to the documents in his possession, custody or control.

[B] Apply for an order that the employer make a further and better list of documents.

[C] Apply for an order that the employer verify his list of documents by affidavit.

[D] Apply for an order for particular discovery.

**11.** Yasmin is claiming damages in the High Court in respect of serious injuries sustained in an accident at work. Does Yasmin have to take out a Summons for Directions?

[A] Yes, because the Rules of Court require the plaintiff to take out a Summons for Directions within one month after pleadings are closed.

[B] Yes, because there are special rules for personal injuries cases, but these do not apply to cases involving employers' liability.

[C] No, because the general rule is that there is no need to seek directions, which are only sought where the facts of the case make it just and expedient.

[D] No, because this is an ordinary personal injuries case and automatic directions apply.

**12.** For some years James has purported to exercise a right of way along a path over Lynn's land. Hearing that Lynn intends to build an outbuilding across the path, James has applied on notice for an interlocutory injunction. Which one of the following propositions best describes the relevance or otherwise of the fact that the building work has not yet commenced?

[A] It has no direct relevance to the question whether the injunction should be granted, apart from being part of the factual background.

[B] Its only relevance is as to whether damages would be an adequate remedy to either party.

[C] It is likely to be the decisive factor if the other factors bearing on the convenience of granting the injunction are evenly balanced.

[D] Its only relevance is in deciding whether the proposed injunction is mandatory or prohibitory.

**13.** In proceedings commenced by general form originating summons, when is the plaintiff required to serve his or her affidavit evidence on the defendants?

[A] At the same time as the originating summons is served on each defendant.

[B] On each defendant within 14 days of that defendant acknowledging service.

[C] On each defendant at least 14 days before the return day of the Master's appointment.

[D] After the Master's appointment in accordance with directions made by the Master on that appointment.

**14.** Anthony is claiming damages for personal injuries against Jason. The trial is unlikely to take place within the next 2 years, but Anthony needs to make some urgent purchases to help him cope with his injuries. Jason has denied liability. An application is made for a payment on account of any damages Anthony may be entitled to. Which one of the following describes the test that Anthony must satisfy on his application regarding the merits of his substantive action?

[A] The merits of his action are irrelevant: all that he needs to show is that he has an immediate need for the items to be purchased.

[B] That he has an arguable case on the merits.

[C] That, on the balance of probabilities, he would obtain judgment at trial for substantial damages.

[D] That it is beyond reasonable doubt that he would obtain judgment at trial for substantial damages.

**15.** David is a drummer in a local rock group. He practices his drumming late at night, much to the annoyance of Timothy, his next-door neighbour. On one occasion when Timothy went to David's house to complain about the noise, David punched Timothy. Which one of the following is the advice you should give to Timothy in relation to bringing County Court proceedings against David claiming an injunction in respect of the nuisance and damages for the assault on the assumption that Timothy wishes, if possible, to avoid having two sets of proceedings?

[A] Timothy must issue two separate summonses against David, a fixed date summons for the nuisance claim and a default summons for the assault claim, because the claims are not of the same or a similar nature.

[B] Timothy must issue a fixed date summons in the nuisance claim and a separate default summons in the assault claim, and may then apply for the actions to be consolidated in a single fixed date action.

[C] Timothy may apply ex parte to the District Judge for leave to issue a single fixed date Summons.

[D] Timothy may simply issue a single fixed date summons.

**16.** On 7 December 1994, Sara issued and served by personal service a generally indorsed writ against Freida claiming damages for breach of contract. Freida has acknowledged service stating that she does not intend to defend the action. It is now 19 December 1994 and Sara asks for your advice on obtaining judgment. In these circumstances, which one of the following is the most appropriate advice to give her?

[A] Sara can enter judgment in default under RSC Ord. 13 immediately.

[B] Sara can enter judgment in default under RSC Ord. 13 only after 21 December 1994.

[C] Sara must serve her Statement of Claim on Freida, and can then apply for judgment in default of Defence under RSC Ord. 19 if Freida fails to serve a Defence within 14 days thereafter.

[D] Sara must serve her Statement of Claim on Freida and may then apply for Summary Judgment under RSC Ord. 14.

**17.** Claude owns a large international pharmaceutical business of long standing based in Switzerland. Most of his trade is with the Far East, although he has a small number of dealings in England. Theresa has commenced County Court proceedings in London against Claude claiming £14,000 under a contract of sale governed by English law. A fully pleaded Defence was served 5 weeks ago alleging that the goods delivered were not of the required quality. Insurance monies in respect of another matter have recently become payable to Claude in London. One hour ago Claude received a telex in Switzerland to the effect that an order had been obtained by Theresa from Mr Justice Green restraining him from removing any of his assets from England, save in so far as they exceed £14,000, until judgment or further order. His London solicitors are now consulting you by telephone. Which one of the following is the best advice to give Claude?

[A] To press the insurance company for payment before they are notified of the order.

[B] To apply for the order to be discharged on the ground that, proceedings having been served, notice of the application to Mr Justice Green should have been given to Claude.

[C] To apply for the order to be discharged on the ground that Claude is not the sort of defendant against whom such an order should be made.

[D] To apply for the order to be discharged on the ground that such an order cannot be made after service of a fully pleaded Defence.

**18**.  As a general rule, answers given by a witness under cross-examination to questions concerning collateral matters must be treated as final. Which of the following is NOT one of the exceptions to the rule?

[A]  Where the witness denics bias towards one of the parties.

[B]  Where the testimony of the witness is unfavourable to the case of the party calling that witness.

[C]  Where the witness denies he has any previous convictions.

[D]  Where the witness denies that he suffers from some physical or mental disability that affects the reliability of his evidence.

**19**.  The following statements all refer to discharging the legal burden in civil cases. Which one is INCORRECT?

[A]  The more serious the allegation the more cogent is the evidence required to overcome the unlikelihood of what is alleged and thus to prove it.

[B]  If the tribunal can say 'We think it more probable than not', or if the probabilities are equal, then the burden is discharged, but nothing short of that will suffice.

[C]  Facts in issue must be proved by a preponderance of probability.

[D]  If the tribunal can say 'We think it more probable than not', the burden is discharged but, if the probabilities are equal, it is not.

**20.** Marcus was injured during the course of his employment with 5-X Brewery Ltd, when the rung of a ladder on which he was required to stand when loading crates of lager collapsed, causing him to fall to the floor and damage his back. In his action for damages against his employers he alleged, inter alia, that his place of work was not kept safe. Section 29(1) of the Factories Act 1961 states 'every place at which any person has at any time to work . . . shall, so far as is reasonably practicable, be made and kept safe for any person working therein'. Who bears the evidential and legal burdens on the issue of whether it was 'reasonably practicable'?

[A] Marcus bears the evidential and legal burden.
[B] Marcus bears the legal burden; 5-X bears the evidential burden.
[C] 5-X bears the evidential and legal burden.
[D] 5-X bears the legal burden; Marcus bears the evidential burden.


**21.** Charles went on a world cruise lasting 9 months. He embarked on 1 January 1985. He was then aged 70 and in a state of poor health. In civil proceedings in 1993 the question arose whether Charles was dead. The Court was satisfied, on the evidence, that since 1985 extensive enquiries and advertisements in various countries had been made by Charles's friends and relatives but that no one had seen or heard from him since he embarked on the cruise. Under the presumption of death, what should the Court presume?

[A] That Charles died on 1 January 1985.
[B] That Charles died on some day between 1 January 1985 and 1 January 1992.
[C] That Charles died on 1 January 1992.
[D] That Charles is dead.

**22.** Printers Inc., a publisher, bring an action against another publisher M & N Ltd for infringement of copyright. M & N Ltd admit that there are strong similarities between passages in one of their recent publications, 'Dieting Daily', and passages in a book, 'Daily Diets', in which Printers Inc. own the copyright, but allege that these similarities are purely coincidental. At the trial, Printers Inc. wish to adduce evidence of three other books published by M & N Ltd which bear strong similarities to books in which other publishing houses own the copyright. The trial judge should:

[A] Exclude the evidence, because Printers Inc. have not alleged fraud or dishonesty.

[B] Exclude the evidence, because it is insufficiently relevant to the facts in issue.

[C] Admit the evidence, because of its relevance to the issue whether the similarities between 'Dieting Daily' and 'Daily Diets' are merely coincidental or due to copying.

[D] Admit the evidence, because of its relevance in showing that M & N Ltd have a disposition to commit conduct of the kind alleged.

**23.** Which of the following propositions concerning the law of evidence in CIVIL proceedings is INCORRECT?

[A] Questions relating to the law of any jurisdiction other than England and Wales are issues of fact to be decided on the evidence given with respect to that law, by the judge.

[B] At common law a judge has no discretionary power to exclude evidence which is relevant and admissible as a matter of law on the ground that it may have been unlawfully obtained.

[C] Evidence of the character of a party or a witness is admissible only if it is among the facts in issue.

[D] The appropriate standard of proof in proceedings for committal to prison arising out of a civil contempt of Court is proof beyond reasonable doubt.

**24**. During the course of the evidence-in-chief of Charles, a witness for the plaintiff, the trial judge grants leave to counsel for the plaintiff to treat Charles as a hostile witness. Counsel for the PLAINTIFF now wishes to do the following:

(i) With the leave of the judge, prove that Charles has made a previous inconsistent statement (under the Criminal Procedure Act 1865, s. 3).

(ii) Ask Charles about a conviction which is recorded against him for perjury.

(iii) Adduce evidence to show that Charles is biased against the plaintiff.

Which of these, if any, should the judge permit?

**[A]** None of them.
**[B]** (i) but not (ii) or (iii).
**[C]** (i) and (ii) but not (iii).
**[D]** (ii) and (iii) but not (i).

**25**. John is suing ABC Ltd, claiming damages for breach of warranty, or alternatively for fraud. John took delivery of a boiler for his new restaurant. On the night he first opened the restaurant to the public, the boiler blew up and his specially invited guests were unable to dine. John alleges that one of the directors of ABC Ltd had represented to him that the boiler had been specially reconditioned and was as good as new, and that there was clearly a fraudulent misrepresentation because the director knew the boiler had not been reconditioned. What standard of proof is appropriate at the trial?

**[A]** On a balance of probabilities for breach of warranty and fraud.

**[B]** Beyond reasonable doubt for breach of warranty and fraud.

**[C]** On a balance of probabilities for the breach of warranty but beyond reasonable doubt for the fraud.

**[D]** Beyond reasonable doubt for the breach of warranty but on a balance of probabilities for the fraud.

**26.** Mary is the Plaintiff in an action against her employers, Mane-Line Hairdressers, for damages for personal injuries sustained during the course of her employment as an apprentice. She claims that her scalp was burned and substantial quantities of her hair fell out when she was experimenting at the salon with some new permanent-wave lotion. In their defence, Mane-Line Hairdressers deny any liability and allege that Mary, having been instructed that apprentices were not to use any of the equipment without supervision, was acting in an unauthorised manner. This allegation is set out in Mane-Line Hairdressers' pleadings, and denied by Mary. If the matter comes to trial, how will the Court regard this allegation?

[A]  As a collateral matter.
[B]  As a preliminary matter.
[C]  As a fact in issue.
[D]  As a fact of which the judge should take judicial notice.

**27.**  Which of the following propositions is INCORRECT?

[A]  A child may give unsworn evidence in civil proceedings.
[B]  A spouse of a party to civil proceedings is competent to testify for that party.
[C]  A spouse of a party to civil proceedings is not competent to testify against that party.
[D]  It is possible for a competent and compellable witness in civil proceedings to refuse to answer specific questions on the grounds of privilege.

**28.**  Which of the following presumptions is NOT capable of putting either a legal or evidential burden on the party against whom it operates?

[A]  The presumption of legitimacy.
[B]  The presumption of continuance of life.
[C]  The presumption of formal validity of a marriage.
[D]  The presumption of death.

**29.** Consider the following types of statement.

(i) A previous inconsistent statement made by a person called as a witness and proved, by virtue of s. 4 or s. 5 of the Criminal Procedure Act 1865, in cross-examination.

(ii) A previous statement made by a person called as a witness and proved for the purpose of rebutting a suggestion that that witness's evidence has been recently fabricated.

(iii) A statement in a document, made by a person called as a witness and used to refresh that witness's memory, which, by reason of cross-examination on the document, is made evidence in the proceedings.

In CIVIL proceedings, which of these statements is admissible as evidence of any fact stated therein?

[A] The statements in (i) and (ii) but not (iii).
[B] The statements in (ii) and (iii) but not (i).
[C] The statements in (i) and (iii) but not (ii).
[D] The statements in (i), (ii) and (iii).

**30.** Harold is suing Frank for fraudulent misrepresentation alleging that Frank sold him a fake diamond ring by representing that the diamond was genuine. Frank defends the action claiming that he mistakenly believed the diamond was genuine. Harold wishes to prove that on several previous occasions over a period of several years Frank had sold fake diamond rings having represented them to be genuine.

Such evidence is:

[A] Admissible to show that Frank was not mistaken about the genuineness of the ring.
[B] Admissible to show that Frank is a fraudster of long standing.
[C] Inadmissible because irrelevant.
[D] Inadmissible in the absence of previous convictions for obtaining money by deception.

**31.** You represent Samantha who consents to summary trial on a charge of receiving stolen goods. You intend to call Samantha herself and a character witness. You can:

[A]  Make both an opening and a closing speech as of right.

[B]  Make an opening speech, and then apply to the magistrates to allow you to make a closing speech as well.

[C]  Make only a closing speech since the only witness whom you are calling other than the accused is not a witness of fact.

[D]  Make only a closing speech since in a summary trial the defence cannot make an opening speech.

**32.** Gerald is arrested in connection with the murder of Harriet. He has been informed of his rights. He has now been lawfully detained for a period of 96 hours. The investigation is not yet complete, and the police wish to detain him for further questioning. In these circumstances, the investigating officers must:

[A]  Take him before a Magistrates' Court who may authorise detention for a further 36 hours.

[B]  Obtain authorisation from an officer of not less than the rank of superintendent, who may authorise detention for a further 6 hours.

[C]  Release him or charge him.

[D]  Release him on bail and then re-arrest him for the murder of Harriet.

**33.** Here are 4 separate situations involving Mike (aged 15). In the first 3, he appears in Court with Neville (aged 18). Only summary offences are involved. Mike and Neville always plead Not Guilty.

In which one of the following situations does the adult Magistrates' Court have NO discretion to send Mike to the Youth Court for trial?

[A] Neville appears in the Magistrates' Court with Mike. Mike is charged with driving whilst disqualified, Neville is charged with aiding and abetting him.

[B] Mike and Neville appear in the Magistrates' Court jointly charged with taking a car without the owner's consent.

[C] Mike and Neville appear in the Magistrates' Court on two separate charges. Neville is alleged to have taken a car without the owner's consent; Mike is accused of allowing himself to be carried in the car, knowing it had been taken without consent.

[D] Mike appears alone in the Magistrates' Court to be tried on a charge of fare-dodging on the London Underground. The magistrates start the trial under the mistaken impression that Mike is 18 years old but then discover his true age.

**34.** Barnabas is convicted in the Magistrates' Court of obtaining property by deception. He appeals against conviction to the Crown Court. The appeal should be heard by:

[A] A Judge sitting alone.

[B] A Judge and a jury.

[C] A Judge sitting with two lay magistrates.

[D] Three Judges.

**35.** Daniel is charged with taking a motor vehicle without the consent of the owner, and Edward is charged, in a separate information, with allowing himself to be carried in it. They do not wish to be tried together. Your advice to them should be that:

[A] As both offences arise out of the same incident, they will be tried together automatically.

[B] They cannot be tried together unless they both agree.

[C] As this is not a joint charge, there will automatically be separate trials.

[D] They will be tried together if the magistrates decide that the offences are so related to each other that a joint trial is necessary in the interests of justice.

**36.** Frank is charged with criminal damage and burglary. The facts alleged by the prosecution are that Frank broke a window, valued at £75 (the criminal damage) to gain access to property from which he stole various specified items (the burglary). In these circumstances:

[A] Frank may elect trial on indictment for the burglary, but the criminal damage must be tried summarily.

[B] Frank may elect trial on indictment for both offences.

[C] Frank has no right to elect trial on indictment.

[D] Frank may elect trial on indictment for the burglary, and the criminal damage may be included, by the prosecution, in the indictment.

**37.** Frank is committed to Barchester Crown Court to stand trial on a charge of burglary. He fails to attend Court on the date fixed for his trial. He is charged with the offence of failing without reasonable cause to surrender to custody, under the Bail Act 1976, s. 6. Which of the following statements about the Bail Act offence is correct?

[A] The offence should be dealt with at the Crown Court by a Judge sitting alone.
[B] The offence should be dealt with at the Crown Court by a Judge sitting with a jury.
[C] The offence should be dealt with at the Crown Court by a Judge sitting with 2 magistrates.
[D] The offence is a purely summary one and so must be dealt with by the Magistrates' Court.

**38.** Alan was charged with assault occasioning actual bodily harm. He was not legally represented. When the charge was put to him in the Magistrates' Court, he said 'Guilty but I was acting in my own defence'. After hearing mitigation the magistrates proceeded to sentence him. Alan subsequently asks you for advice on appeal. You should advise:

[A] He can appeal against conviction to the Crown Court which may acquit Alan if the plea was equivocal.
[B] He can appeal against sentence only as he pleaded guilty.
[C] He can appeal against conviction to the Crown Court which may hear the appeal themselves, by way of a retrial.
[D] He can appeal against conviction to the Crown Court on the basis that the plea was equivocal and the Crown Court may remit the case to the magistrates to rehear on a not guilty plea.

**39.** Idris (aged 15) is found guilty in the Youth Court of committing a burglary involving the theft of £25,000 worth of jewellery. He is now due to be sentenced for the crime. Which of the following propositions is correct?

The Youth Court:

[A] May commit him for sentence to the Crown Court.
[B] Must deal with him itself.
[C] Must commit him for sentence to the Crown Court.
[D] May commit him for sentence to the adult Magistrates' Court.

**40.** Francesca (aged 22) is convicted of theft by the Greenbridge Magistrates' Court. Being of the opinion that the offence is so serious that greater punishment should be inflicted for the offence than they have power to impose, the Greenbridge magistrates commit her for sentence under the Magistrates' Courts Act 1980, s. 38, to the Pencaster Crown Court. The Pencaster Crown Court imposes a sentence of 3 months' imprisonment. Francesca now wishes to appeal to the Court of Appeal against sentence.

Which one of the following statements is correct?

[A] Francesca may appeal as of right.
[B] Francesca may appeal with leave of the single judge of the Court of Appeal.
[C] Francesca may appeal with leave of the sentencing judge.
[D] Francesca cannot appeal to the Court of Appeal.

**41.** Nicky is aged 14. He appears in the Youth Court, charged alone with several burglaries of dwelling houses (such burglary being punishable with up to 14 years' imprisonment following conviction on indictment in the case of an adult offender). The value of property stolen in the burglaries is over £20,000. The Youth Court decides to hold committal proceedings, with a view to committing Nicky to the Crown Court for trial.

Assuming there is a prima facie case against Nicky, which one of the following statements is correct?

[A] He can be committed for trial because a Crown Court judge might lawfully pass a sentence under s. 53(2) of the Children and Young Persons Act 1933.
[B] He must be committed for trial because the offences are too serious for magistrates to deal with.
[C] He cannot be committed for trial because he is not charged together with an adult and a sentence under s. 53(2) of the Children and Young Persons Act 1933 is not lawful in his case.
[D] He cannot be committed for trial because juveniles cannot be tried in the Crown Court for burglary.

**42.** James fails to attend his summary trial for an offence of theft by shoplifting. At his last appearance before the Court on that charge, he was told of the time and date of his trial. The magistrates:

[A] Must adjourn the case until James is present.
[B] Have a discretion to hear the case on the basis of a not guilty plea.
[C] Must proceed to hear the case on the basis of a not guilty plea.
[D] Must proceed to deal with the case and, as James has failed to appear, have a discretion as to whether to treat him as if he had pleaded guilty.

**43.** Jacob is arrested in connection with an offence of robbery, and, on Jacob's arrival at the Police Station, a decision to detain him is made at 8 am by Police Constable Brown, who is not involved in the investigation. Reviews of detention are held by Sergeant Green at 2 pm and 11 pm. Jacob is given substantial meals at 12.30 pm and 6 pm and short breaks in the interrogation every two hours. He has now been in custody for 23 hours without charge, and consults a solicitor. What advice should his solicitor give him about his detention?

[A] The detention should have been reviewed at 2 pm, 8 pm and 2 am.

[B] The detention should have been reviewed at 2 pm, 8 pm and 2 am, and those reviews and their original decision to detain should have been carried out by officers of higher ranks.

[C] The times of the reviews are correct but those reviews, and the original decision to detain, should have been carried out by officers of higher ranks.

[D] He has no ground of complaint.


**44.** Kevin is convicted in the Magistrates' Court of burglary. He now wishes to apply for judicial review. In order to do so, he must *first*:

[A] Serve notice on the Magistrates' Court and on the High Court of his intention to apply for judicial review.

[B] Apply to the High Court for leave to make the application for judicial review.

[C] Serve his application for judicial review on the Magistrates' Court, the High Court and the prosecution.

[D] Issue a summons against the prosecution to appear in the High Court.

**45**. Harry elects summary trial on a charge of assault occasioning actual bodily harm. He is found guilty and fined. He wishes to appeal against conviction, but not against sentence. He asks you for advice as to any adverse implications for him. You should advise him that the Crown Court:

[A] Can order him to pay the prosecution's costs but cannot increase the sentence.

[B] Cannot order him to pay the prosecution's costs nor increase his sentence.

[C] Can order him to pay the prosecution's costs and can increase the sentence to the maximum which the magistrates could have imposed.

[D] Can order him to pay the prosecution's costs and can increase the sentence to the maximum which the Crown Court could have imposed if he had been tried on indictment.

**46.** Gareth, a Welsh nationalist, is charged with the murder of Harry, an English motorist. The prosecution case is that Gareth, while standing on a bridge over a busy road, rolled a granite boulder over the edge and onto the road; and that the boulder fell through the windscreen of Harry's car, causing him multiple injuries from which he died within minutes. Gareth gives evidence admitting these facts but denying that he intended to cause death or serious bodily harm to Harry. Which would be the best way in which to direct the jury on the question of whether they may infer that Gareth intended death or serious bodily harm as a result of his actions?

[A] 'You should decide whether Gareth intended death or serious bodily harm by reference to all the evidence, drawing such inferences as appear proper in the circumstances.'

[B] 'You are not entitled to infer that Gareth intended death or serious bodily harm as a result of his actions.'

[C] 'If you are satisfied that death or serious bodily harm was a natural and probable consequence of Gareth's actions, then you should infer that he intended death or serious bodily harm as a result of those actions.'

[D] 'You may only infer that Gareth intended death or serious bodily harm as a result of his actions if he has failed to satisfy you that he did not intend death or serious bodily harm.'

**47.** Jane is charged on indictment with obtaining property by deception from Harrods, having ordered goods on a credit account using a false name. At the trial, counsel for Jane, on her behalf, admits that she had opened this account, Can the prosecution rely on counsel's admission.

[A] No, because the admission was not in writing.

[B] Yes, because the admission was made orally in Court.

[C] No, because counsel's admission can never bind Jane.

[D] Yes, because although the admission is inadmissible, the judge will exercise his discretion to admit it.

**48.** Fred and Harry are jointly charged with blackmailing their employer. Fred pleads not guilty; Harry pleads guilty. The prosecution wish to call Fred's wife, Ghisha, and Harry's wife, Irene, to give evidence. Are Ghisha and Irene competent and compellable to give evidence for the prosecution?

[A] Ghisha is competent and compellable; Irene is competent but not compellable.

[B] Ghisha is competent but not compellable; Irene is competent and compellable.

[C] Both Ghisha and Irene are competent but not compellable.

[D] Both Ghisha and Irene are competent and compellable.


**49.** At a trial on indictment, the jury, after an hour's retirement to consider their verdict, return to the Court. The foreman tells the judge that a number of the jurors have expressed their difficulty in deciding whether the prosecution have discharged the burden of proof because they do not understand the meaning of proof 'beyond reasonable doubt'. Which of the following would be the best way for the judge to respond?

[A] 'I cannot help you, because if I attempted any gloss upon the words, or were to give you an analogy, it might be misleading.'

[B] 'It means exactly what it says: a doubt for which one could give reasons if asked.'

[C] 'It means the sort of doubt which might affect you in the conduct of your everyday affairs.'

[D] 'It means the kind of doubt which, when you are dealing with matters of importance in your own affairs, you allow to influence you one way or the other.'

**50.** Michael is charged with indecently assaulting Nora. The case for the prosecution is that he and Nora were sitting together in a train travelling from London to Oxford and that shortly after the train passed through Reading, Michael put out his hand and touched Nora's breasts. Michael admits that he and Nora were sitting together in the train, but denies that he touched her. When the police (lawfully) searched Michael's briefcase they discovered a number of pornographic magazines containing pictures of naked women. Will evidence of this discovery be admitted at Michael's trial?

[A] Yes, because it is evidence of Michael's lustful disposition.

[B] Yes, because it rebuts Michael's denial of the offence.

[C] No, because any probative value it may have is outweighed by its prejudicial effect.

[D] No, because although highly relevant, it should be excluded under s. 78 of the Police and Criminal Evidence Act 1984.

**51.** Carlos is charged with murder and raises the defence of diminished responsibility. Which party bears the evidential and legal burdens in relation to the defence raised; and what standard of proof is required to discharge the legal burden on that defence?

[A] The evidential burden is on the defence; the legal burden is on the prosecution and will be discharged by proof beyond reasonable doubt.

[B] The evidential burden is on the defence; the legal burden is also on the defence and will be discharched by raising a reasonable doubt.

[C] The evidential burden is on the defence; the legal burden is also on the defence and will be discharged by proof on a balance of probabilities.

[D] The evidential burden is on the prosecution; the legal burden is on the defence and will be discharged by proof beyond reasonable doubt.

**52.** Which of the following propositions concerning defence cross-examination in rape offence cases is INCORRECT?

[A] No questions can be asked about the complainant's sexual relations with persons other than the accused without leave of the judge.

[B] Application for leave to cross-examine about the complainant's sexual relations with persons other than the accused must be made in the jury's absence.

[C] Application for leave to cross-examine about the complainant's sexual relations with persons other than the accused is only necessary where the accused puts forward the defence of consent or honest belief in consent.

[D] In determining whether such leave should be granted the judge has to consider whether it is more likely than not that the proposed cross-examination might reasonably lead the jury to take a different view of the complainant's evidence from that which they might take if the cross-examination were not allowed.

**53.** Tom, who has previous convictions for offences of dishonesty, is charged with burglary. He does not give evidence but his counsel puts to the chief witness for the prosecution that he (the witness) has 2 previous convictions for theft, as in fact is the case. The witness denies that he has such convictions. Which of the following propositions about these circumstances is INCORRECT?

[A] It is a matter of discretion for the judge whether to make a comment in his summing-up on Tom's failure to give evidence.

[B] Counsel for the prosecution may make a formal admission that the witness has the 2 convictions for theft.

[C] Counsel for the defence may prove the fact of the convictions for theft.

[D] Tom has put his character in issue and the prosecution, with the leave of the judge, may call evidence of Tom's previous convictions.

**54.** Lawrence is charged with murder, and relies on the defence of self-defence. Shortly after the incident, he told Malcolm, a friend, that his defence would be one of self-defence. At the trial, Lawrence gives evidence of self-defence. Consider the following 2 statements:

(i) Lawrence's words to Malcolm are prima facie inadmissible as a previous consistent statement.

(ii) Lawrence's words to Malcolm are admissible if the prosecution put it to Lawrence that he has invented the defence only after hearing the prosecution case to serve his own purposes at the trial.

Which of the above statements is correct?

[A] Only (i).
[B] Only (ii).
[C] Neither.
[D] Both.


**55.** Which of the following statements best describes the position at trial where a witness has previously identified the accused out of Court?

[A] Evidence of the out-of-Court identification is inadmissible.

[B] Evidence of the out-of-Court identification is admissible, but only after the witness has identified the accused in Court.

[C] Evidence of the out-of-Court identification is admissible, but only if the witness has been unable to identify the accused in Court.

[D] Evidence of the out-of-Court identification is admissible and this should be elicited prior to the witness identifying the accused in Court.

**56**. Alf is charged with the murder of a woman cyclist by deliberately driving his car at her. The prosecution can prove that in the week before the alleged murder, in separate incidents Alf had knocked 2 other women cyclists off their bicycles. Alf's defence is accident. The evidence of the other incidents is:

[A] Inadmissible because its prejudicial effect outweighs its probative value.
[B] Inadmissible because it is irrelevant.
[C] Admissible because its probative value outweighs its prejudicial effect.
[D] Admissible because similar fact evidence is always admissible to rebut a defence of accident.


**57**. Tom is charged with a series of thefts of Volkswagen 'Beetle' cars on 3 different occasions. Following a search of Tom's garden and garage, where pieces of cars were discovered and identified as coming from the stolen vehicles, the police interviewed Tom's wife, Jane. Jane made a statement to the police in which she admitted that Tom had an obsession for this type of vehicle and was hoping to create a perfect 'Beetle' out of spare parts taken from other similar cars. Jane and Tom separated for some weeks during which time the committal proceedings took place at which Jane gave evidence for the prosecution. By the time of Tom's trial, Tom and Jane were reconciled and Jane refused to testify. When called upon by the prosecution to take the oath, is Jane competent *and* compellable?

[A] Yes, because she has already given a witness statement to the police.
[B] No, she is incompetent because she is Tom's spouse and has not yet been sworn.
[C] No, she is competent but not compellable.
[D] Yes, because she gave evidence at the committal proceedings.

**58.** John and his wife Michelle have been living apart for the past 2 years. Michelle decided to refuse John any further access to the 2 children aged 8 and 10, as the children told her that their father was drunk and violent on the last 2 visits. On being refused access, John turned up at Michelle's house where he assaulted her and the children. In subsequent criminal proceedings the prosecution intend to call Michelle as the main prosecution witness. She is reluctant to testify as she is frightened of John. Is Michelle competent *and* compellable for the prosecution?

[A]  Yes, because Michelle is separated from John.
[B]  Yes, because of the nature of the offences concerned.
[C]  No, because although competent Michelle is not compellable.
[D]  No, because they are still married and she is neither competent nor compellable.


**59.** Morgan is charged with indecently assaulting a 9-year-old girl in the town park at 4 pm on 11 September last year. His defence is mistaken identity. He told the police officer investigating the incident that he left work early that day in order to accompany his wife to the health clinic but did not get home until after she had left because he missed the bus. At trial, he testifies that, after he had missed the bus, he took a short cut through the town park that afternoon; and that he omitted to state this to the officer because he had been in trouble with the police before and he was afraid that 'they would try to pin things on him again'. The judge allows the prosecution to cross-examine Morgan on his previous conviction for indecent exposure. *On the facts given*, the best justification for this ruling is that:

[A]  He is not a credible witness.
[B]  He has cast imputations on the character of a prosecution witness.
[C]  He has already revealed his character to the jury.
[D]  The previous conviction shows a general propensity towards offences of a sexual nature.

**60**. Owen is charged with burglary from premises owned by Melanie. He has a previous conviction for theft. Melanie, while giving evidence for the prosecution, says Owen is a complete stranger to her. Owen, in his evidence, explains his presence in the house, where his fingerprints were found, by saying that he was having an affair with Melanie and that she has denied all knowledge of him because she does not want her husband to know. As a matter of law (i.e. ignoring any question of discretion) can the judge allow the prosecution to cross-examine Owen as to his previous conviction?

[A] Yes, because his previous conviction of an offence of dishonesty shows that he is disposed to commit such offences.

[B] Yes, because he has cast imputations on the character of a prosecution witness.

[C] No, because he has not cast any imputation on the character of a prosecution witness.

[D] No, because Owen's allegations against Melanie were necessary to enable him to establish his defence.

# MCT – Part 2

# [TIME LIMIT: 3 HOURS]

### CIVIL LITIGATION

**1.** Richard, who owns a garden centre, purchased some catalogues from Barchester Printing Limited. The catalogues, which were supplied in September 1988, were very poorly printed. Richard served a writ in July 1994. In October 1994 Barchester served a Defence alleging that the contract was made not with it but with Barchester Printing (1982) Limited, a different company but with the same registered office. It is now March 1995 and Richard wishes to amend his writ and Statement of Claim by substituting Barchester Printing (1982) Limited for Barchester Printing Limited. Which one of the following correctly describes the principle that will be applied by the Court?

[A] Richard's application may be granted if he can show he made a genuine mistake as to the name of the defendant and that his mistake was not misleading.
[B] Richard's application may be granted because the companies have the same registered office.
[C] Richard's application cannot be granted because the Court has no jurisdiction to allow such an amendment once the limitation period has expired.
[D] Richard's application cannot be granted unless he can show that Barchester deliberately tried to mislead him as to the identity of the contracting party.

**2.** On a taxation of costs on the standard basis, which one of the following principles should be applied?

[A] There should be allowed all costs except in so far as they are of an unreasonable amount or have been unreasonably incurred, any doubts being resolved in favour of the receiving party.

[B] The Court shall have an unfettered discretion as to the items of expenditure to be allowed and as to the amount to be allowed in respect of such items.

[C] The party paying the costs shall not be ordered to pay more than such amount (if any) as is reasonable having regard to the financial circumstances of all the parties and their conduct in connection with the dispute.

[D] There should be allowed a reasonable amount in respect of all costs reasonably incurred, any doubts being resolved in favour of the paying party.

**3.** After judgment has been obtained in the High Court, which one of the following methods of enforcement is not executed by the sheriff?

[A] Seizure and sale of the judgment debtor's goods in satisfaction of a money judgment.

[B] Seizure of listed and identified goods for delivery to the plaintiff.

[C] Attaching a debt due from a third party to the judgment debtor so that the third party is required to pay the debt direct to the judgment creditor.

[D] Removal of persons from land and giving possession to the plaintiff.

**4.** The plaintiff alleges that goods delivered on 3 June 1989 under a contract were not of merchantable quality. A writ issued in London on 30 November 1994 was sent by ordinary first-class post to the defendant's last known address on 6 March 1995, but was returned today, Wednesday 29 March 1995, marked 'Gone away'. What immediate action should the plaintiff take?

[A] Make every effort to find the defendant and, if possible, effect personal service today.

[B] Issue a fresh writ today and effect service in the usual way in due course.

[C] Lodge an affidavit in Central Office today setting out the history of the case and asking for an order extending the validity of the writ.

[D] Issue a summons today supported by an affidavit seeking an order extending the validity of the writ.

**5.** Which one of the following best describes a writ of *subpoena duces tecum*?

[A] It is a High Court command to a witness to attend Court to give oral testimony only.

[B] It is a High Court command to a witness to attend Court to produce documents.

[C] It is a County Court command to a witness to attend Court to give oral testimony only.

[D] It is a County Court command to a witness to attend Court to produce documents.

**6.** Magic Makeup Plc, an English company, contracted to buy a quantity of lipsticks from Daisy Bell Products Inc., an American company incorporated in New York. By its terms, English law is to govern the contract. The contract also contains a jurisdiction clause which states 'the High Court in London shall have jurisdiction to determine any disputes arising out of this contract'. Daisy Bell Inc. have considerable assets in England. Magic Makeup now want to sue Daisy Bell for breach of contract in the High Court in London. Magic Makeup should be advised:

[A] That the English Courts have jurisdiction by virtue of the fact that the plaintiffs (i.e. Magic Makeup) are incorporated in England.

[B] That they should seek leave from the High Court to issue and serve a writ on Daisy Bell in the USA.

[C] That they can serve a writ on Daisy Bell in the USA without leave.

[D] That they will have to sue Daisy Bell in New York, as, due to the fact that Daisy Bell are incorporated there, those Courts have sole jurisdiction.


**7.** Winston is suing Laura for damages for an alleged breach of contract committed on 7 December 1992. Laura served Winston with a Request for Further and Better Particulars of the Statement of Claim on 6 April 1994, and the Master made an order on the summons for directions on 20 December 1994 requiring Winston to provide those Particulars within the next 21 days. It is now 29 March 1995, and Winston has not yet served the Particulars. Which one of the following orders is most likely to be made upon an application by Laura?

[A] An 'unless' order in respect of the Further and Better Particulars.

[B] An order dismissing the action on the grounds of inordinate and inexcusable delay.

[C] An order striking out the Statement of Claim as an abuse of the process of the Court.

[D] An order that the action be discontinued.

**8.** Jane is suing her employer for damages following an accident when her arm was trapped in the doors of a lift at work. You are instructed to advise Jane whether it is possible to obtain copies of her employer's witnesses' statements before trial. Which one of the following correctly states the situation.

[A] There is jurisdiction to order the exchange of witnesses' statements only in the specialist Courts, such as the Commercial and Admiralty Courts, of the High Court.

[B] Mutual exchange of witnesses' statements is one of the automatic directions in both the High Court and the County Court.

[C] Whether the action is proceeding in the High Court or the County Court, requiring an exchange of witnesses' statements is only possible if an order is made on an application to the Court.

[D] Witnesses' statements are covered by legal professional privilege, and it is not possible to obtain an order for the disclosure of the other side's witnesses' statements.

**9.** A County Court judge gives final judgment in the sum of £5,000 in an action based on an alleged breach of contract. If the defendant wishes to appeal, to which one of the following should the appeal be brought?

[A] The Divisional Court.
[B] A High Court Judge in Chambers.
[C] A High Court Judge sitting in open Court.
[D] The Court of Appeal.

**10.** Pleadings in a personal injuries case closed in July 1993. In January 1994 the plaintiff disclosed, in accordance with RSC Ord. 25, r. 8, a report on his injuries by Mr Brown, a consultant surgeon. After a change of solicitors a more favourable report by Mr Green was disclosed by the plaintiff in November 1994. The case has now come on for trial. Mr Green has been called for the plaintiff, but Mr Brown has not. Mr Brown's report corresponds with a report from Mr White prepared for the defendant. The plaintiff objects to the defendant putting in evidence Mr Brown's report. How should the judge rule on the defendant's application to adduce Mr Brown's report?

[A] That it is inadmissible by virtue of the implied undertaking not to use the report without the consent of the party who disclosed it, in this case the plaintiff.

[B] That it is inadmissible without the plaintiff's consent by virtue of the confidential relationship between doctor and patient.

[C] That it is protected by legal professional privilege, unless the privilege is waived by the plaintiff.

[D] That it is admissible regardless of the consent of the plaintiff.

**11.** Where the Court applies the guidelines in *American Cyanamid* v *Ethicon* (1975) on an application for an interlocutory injunction, which one of the 4 following propositions best describes the degree to which the plaintiff must establish the merits of his case?

[A] The plaintiff must show a strong prima facie case that his rights have been infringed.

[B] The plaintiff must show that there is a serious issue to be tried.

[C] The plaintiff must show that his claim is more likely to succeed than fail at the trial.

[D] The plaintiff must show, on the balance of probabilities, that there is no defence to the action.

**12.** Immediately before the trial of an action commenced by Roger against William, the trial judge makes an order that a question be referred to the European Court. Which one of the following best describes the effect of such a reference?

[A] The English action will be stayed until the European Court has given a preliminary ruling on the referred question, and the English Courts will be bound by that ruling on that question.

[B] The English trial will immediately proceed, and the trial judge will decide all issues apart from the question referred to the European Court. The action will then be adjourned until the European Court has given a ruling on the question, when judgment will be given by the English Court.

[C] Roger and William will be required to agree the facts, which will be annexed to the reference to the European Court in a schedule, and the European Court will then give judgment to Roger or William in accordance with its decision on the question referred.

[D] The English action will be discontinued, and Roger will be required to commence a fresh action before the European Court, which will decide all the issues between the parties and give judgment accordingly.

**13.** In relation to appearances in the County Court, when should counsel ask for a certificate that attendance by counsel was appropriate?

[A] In respect of every appearance.

[B] In respect of all interlocutory applications.

[C] In respect of interlocutory applications where either party is legally aided.

[D] Only in respect of applications heard by the District Judge.

**14.** The plaintiff in a writ action, which is about to be set down for trial, intends to rely at trial on a written statement from a witness who is now seriously ill with a debilitating disease and is unlikely to recover. Which one of the following steps should the plaintiff take?

[A] Serve the defendant with a notice of his intention to give the statement in evidence at the trial complying with RSC Ord. 38, r. 22 and stating that the witness is unfit to attend as a witness by reason of his bodily condition.

[B] Arrange for the witness's evidence to be taken before a Magistrate in a deposition under the provisions of the Magistrates' Courts Act 1980, s. 105, at the witness's hospital bedside if need be.

[C] Delay setting down for trial until after the witness has died, because death is one of the specified reasons justifying not calling a witness at trial under the Civil Evidence Act 1968, and will prevent the defendant serving a counternotice.

[D] Apply by summons to a Master supported by an affidavit deposing to the material facts for an order giving leave to adduce the statement at trial.

**15.** Which one of the following correctly describes the rules on where proceedings claiming the price of goods sold and delivered can be commenced?

[A] Always in a County Court, because claims for the price under a contract are claims for liquidated amounts.

[B] Only in a County Court where the price claimed is below £25,000; otherwise either in the High Court or a County Court.

[C] Either in the High Court or a County Court, irrespective of the amount claimed.

[D] Either in the High Court or a County Court where the amount claimed is below £25,000; otherwise only in the High Court.

**16.** Fast Ltd have commenced proceedings against Slow Ltd claiming damages in tort and for breach of contract in respect of allegedly defective building work. Slow Ltd have paid £15,000 into Court 'in satisfaction of all the causes of action in respect of which the plaintiff claims'. In these circumstances, which one of the following propositions is correct?

[A] When a payment into Court is made where more than one cause of action is alleged, the defendant must allocate specific sums to each cause of action, so Slow Ltd's payment was irregular.

[B] Although Slow Ltd were entitled to make the payment in in the form they used, the Court may order them to specify the sum paid in respect of each cause of action if Fast Ltd have been embarrassed.

[C] Slow Ltd had a choice as to whether to make the payment in in the form they used or by specifying individual sums for each cause of action, and Fast Ltd are not entitled to object to the form chosen.

[D] A payment into Court must be in satisfaction of all the causes of action alleged in the proceedings, so Slow Ltd's payment was in the correct form.

**17**. On 27 February 1989, Duff Aluminium Co. Ltd ('Duff') delivered 30 tons of aluminium components to Peterborough Motor Manufacturing Plc ('Peterborough'). Peterborough paid Duff's invoice, but subsequently alleged that the components were too soft and useless. There has been voluminous correspondence between the parties, and solicitors have been instructed by both sides. Duff say that the soft aluminium identified by Peterborough must have come from another supplier. In December 1994 Peterborough's solicitors informed Duff's solicitors that a protective writ had been issued on 7 November 1994. In a letter dated 4 January 1995, marked 'without prejudice', Duff's solicitors replied:

'While it is denied that the soft aluminium came from our client, our client accepts there is a prospect of a Court finding that in fact it did. We are at present seeking authority from our client as to proposals for settling this dispute, and would be grateful if you would consider postponing service for the time being so as to avoid unnecessary costs being incurred.'

It is now 29 March 1995. The writ has not been served, and the parties have been unable to agree terms despite a number of offers and counter-offers. Which one of the following is the best advice to give to Peterborough?

[A] Simply serving the expired writ and hoping Duff will not take the point that it is no longer valid is not an option, because the limitation period has expired.

[B] As it is marked 'without prejudice', the letter of 4 January 1995 could not be referred to on any application to renew the writ. Therefore Peterborough could only point to continuing negotiations, so any application to extend the validity of the writ would fail.

[C] On the facts there is a good reason for not having served the writ in time, so an application to extend its period of validity should succeed.

[D] Although on the facts there may be a good reason for not having served the writ in time, any application to extend its period of validity will fail unless there is a satisfactory explanation for not making the application before the writ expired.

**18.** William was employed by Domestic Chemicals plc. In April 1990 there was an escape of chemical vapours at the plant where William worked. In January 1991 William attended a routine medical examination, after which he was informed that as a result of the April accident, he had suffered latent damage to his lungs which would fully develop within 2 years. In March 1992 William developed symptoms of bronchial asthma and had to retire. In October 1994 he sought advice from a solicitor, who told him that he had a good cause of action against Domestic Chemicals. A writ was issued later that month. The writ was served in February 1995. You would advise Domestic Chemicals that the date when the limitation period started to run was:

[A]  April 1990.
[B]  January 1991.
[C]  March 1992.
[D]  October 1994.

**19.** Sally, who is in business buying and selling motor cars, has applied for summary judgment under CCR Ord. 9, r. 14 for the sum of £4,000 being the price of a motor car sold to Brian. In his affidavit Brian sets out a long list of defects in the car and says he is refusing to pay on the ground that the car was not of merchantable quality. Exhibited estimates put the cost of curing the defects at £2,500. If Sally does not contest the facts set out in Brian's affidavit, which one of the following orders is the District Judge most likely to make?

[A]  Unconditional leave to defend.
[B]  Conditional leave to defend.
[C]  Judgment for Sally in the sum of £1,500, unconditional leave to defend for the balance.
[D]  Judgment for Sally in the sum of £4,000 subject to a stay of execution in respect of £2,500.

**20**. April Fashions Ltd have served proceedings on Haymarket Insurance Plc claiming insurance monies alleged to be due under a policy after their premises were destroyed by fire. Haymarket have refused payment because they allege the fire was deliberately started by April Fashions' managing director. April Fashions' bank has foreclosed against the site of their former premises. Apart from the unpaid insurance monies April Fashions are clearly insolvent. On Haymarket's application for security for costs the Master considers that both sides have prospects of success at trial, but Haymarket's case is marginally stronger than that of April Fashions. How is the Master likely to deal with the application?

[A]  Grant the order although April Fashions have an arguable claim, because the defendants are more likely to win at trial than April Fashions and April Fashions are clearly insolvent.

[B]  Although he must always disregard the merits of the case, he should grant the order because April Fashions are clearly insolvent.

[C]  Although he must take into account his finding that the defendants are more likely to win at trial than April Fashions, on balance he should refuse the order because the defendants' refusal to pay on the policy had contributed to April Fashions' financial problems and to order them to provide security might stifle a genuine claim.

[D]  He should disregard the merits of the case as they are not sufficiently overwhelming, and refuse the order because the defendants' refusal to pay on the policy contributed to April Fashions' financial problems, and to order them to provide security might stifle a genuine claim.

**21.** You act for Laura, who is funding her case privately, and who is the plaintiff in a boundary dispute action against her neighbour, Martin, who is covered by a full legal aid certificate. At trial the County Court judge decides all issues in favour of Laura. What should you say to the judge on the question of costs?

[A] That in the circumstances Martin should be ordered to pay Laura's costs of the action, not to be enforced without the leave of the Court.

[B] That as Martin is protected on costs by the legal aid certificate, there should be no order as to costs.

[C] That as all issues have been decided in favour of Laura, Martin should be ordered to pay Laura's costs of the action.

[D] That in the circumstances the question as to costs should be adjourned to allow the Legal Aid Board to intervene as you intend to apply for an order that the Legal Aid Board should pay Laura's costs of the action.

**22.** Peter, who is suing Deborah in the High Court, has allowed 3 years to elapse after the close of pleadings without taking any further steps. The limitation period expired a year ago. Peter has now given Deborah 1 month's written notice that he intends to take out a summons for directions without giving any explanation for the delay. Which one of the following is the best advice to give to Deborah?

[A] That Peter needed to give notice of intention to proceed, which he has done, so Deborah can do nothing and the action will now proceed in the usual way.

[B] The limitation period having expired, Peter needs leave to continue the action, which Deborah may oppose on the ground that Peter has no reasonable explanation for the delay.

[C] Deborah now has a Limitation Act defence to Peter's action, and should seek leave to amend her Defence.

[D] Deborah may apply for an order that Peter's action be dismissed on the ground of inordinate and inexcusable delay.

**23.**  Douglas has been served with a document sealed by the High Court which (a) orders him to disclose and deliver up certain specified information and documents; (b) requires him to permit a named supervising solicitor to enter and search his premises and to seize documents; and (c) requires him to verify on oath the information and documents produced under (a). What has been served on Douglas?

[A]  An *Anton Piller* order.

[B]  A *Mareva* injunction.

[C]  A *Norwich Pharmacal* order.

[D]  An order for pre-action discovery under the Supreme Court Act 1981, s. 33(2).

## CIVIL EVIDENCE

**24.**  Philip is suing his employer for damages for negligence and breach of statutory duty arising out of an accident at work in which he was injured while operating a press. The employer is alleging contributory negligence. Immediately after the accident, Quentin, a fellow worker and witness to the accident, went to the foreman, Robert, and said that Philip had failed to follow the correct safety procedures before operating the press. Robert went to his supervisor, Sylvia, and told her what Quentin had said. Sylvia then went to the Safety Officer, Timothy, and told him what Quentin had said.

Assuming compliance with any relevant procedural requirements, which of the following best describes the manner in which Quentin's oral statement may be proved?

[A]  By the evidence of Quentin (in which case, the statement shall not be given in evidence without the leave of the Court).

[B]  As in [A] OR by the evidence of Robert.

[C]  As in [A] OR by the evidence of Robert OR Sylvia.

[D]  As in [A] OR by the evidence of Robert, Sylvia OR Timothy.

**25.** Beneficiaries bring an action against their trustee in the Chancery Division, alleging misuse of trust funds. The trustee is cross-examined as to the spending of the trust monies for his own purposes. He declines to answer, because his answer would incriminate him of the offence of theft.

Which of the following correctly describes the evidential position?

[A] He must not answer.
[B] He can refuse to answer and, if he does, cannot be liable for contempt of Court.
[C] He must answer, but his answer cannot be used against him in the civil proceedings.
[D] He must answer, but his answer cannot be used against him should he subsequently be prosecuted for theft.

**26.** David, a pedestrian, is called for the plaintiff in a negligence action brought to recover the cost of repairs to a motor car involved in a minor accident. David testifies that he saw both cars travelling at about 30 mph, that the defendant's vehicle was no more than 5 yards behind the plaintiff's, and that the defendant failed to stop in time when the plaintiff had to brake suddenly at a zebra crossing. Although he has been a passenger in cars many times, David has never held a driver's licence. David's evidence is:

[A] Inadmissible because he is not qualified as an expert.
[B] Admissible non-expert opinion evidence.
[C] Inadmissible evidence of fact, i.e. evidence containing no statements of opinion.
[D] Inadmissible because it relates, in part, to the ultimate issues in the case.

**27.** Priscilla is suing Damien in the High Court. Within 21 days of the case having been set down for trial, she serves a notice under RSC Ord. 38, r. 21 indicating her desire to give in evidence, for the truth of its contents, a statement of fact made by Edward and admissible in evidence under the Civil Evidence Act 1968, s. 2. Edward is employed by Damien but his statement was not authorised, expressly or otherwise, by Damien. In the notice, Priscilla does not state that Edward cannot or should not be called as a witness. Damien, within 21 days after service of the notice on him, serves on Priscilla a counter-notice requiring her to call Edward as a witness at the trial. Priscilla does not call Edward, who is still employed by Damien. At the trial, the question arises whether Edward's statement (assuming that it can lawfully be proved) is admissible for the truth of its contents.

What should the judge do?

[A] The judge should exclude the statement because Priscilla has failed to comply with a counter-notice duly served on her.

[B] Notwithstanding Priscilla's failure to comply with the counter-notice duly served on her, the judge should consider whether to admit the statement as a matter of discretion.

[C] The judge should exclude the statement because it was not authorised by Damien.

[D] The judge should admit the statement because it is an informal admission made by someone in privity with Damien and therefore admissible without compliance with the notice procedure.

**28.** In the course of a contractual dispute between Dick and Peter, Dick sent Peter a letter marked 'Private and Confidential' in which he disputed liability but offered Peter 50% of the amount he was claiming as due to him. Peter declined this offer and is now suing. Dick in his defence denies any liability. Peter would like to put Dick's letter in evidence. Dick objects. The judge should rule that:

[A] The letter is admissible against Dick because it was not marked 'without prejudice'.

[B] The letter has no relevance to Dick's liability and is inadmissible for that reason.

[C] The letter is inadmissible because it should be treated as if written without prejudice.

[D] The letter is inadmissible because its prejudice is greater than its probative value.


**29.** Raymond issues a writ against Steve, claiming damages for injuries which Raymond suffered when their cars collided at a crossroads. Raymond alleges that Steve was negligent. Raymond pleads in his Statement of Claim that Steve has been convicted by the local Magistrates' Court of driving carelessly at the time of their collision. Steve serves a Defence, denying negligence and claiming that the conviction was erroneous.

On the issue of Steve's negligence, which one of the following statements best describes the legal position?

[A] Raymond must prove Steve's negligence.

[B] Raymond must prove Steve's negligence and will raise a rebuttable presumption of this by proving Steve's conviction.

[C] Whether Raymond proves Steve's conviction or not, Steve must prove he was not negligent.

[D] Raymond must prove Steve's negligence and will do so conclusively by proving Steve's conviction.

**30.** Jason, whilst receiving radiation treatment from some newly-installed equipment in an NHS hospital, was given a serious overdose. When Jason indicated that he would sue the Hospital Authority, the Authority contacted the equipment manufacturers, who asked the Authority for a report from the technician in charge. The technician supplied a report to the Authority. They sent one copy to the manufacturers and another to their solicitors. Jason who is now suing the Hospital Authority wants discovery of the report, but the Authority are claiming privilege for it, saying that one of its purposes was to get legal advice in case they were sued. Are they entitled to withhold the report?

[A]  No, if the main purpose of the report was to find out what went wrong and to prevent it in future.

[B]  No, because it was from the technician to his employers and therefore not a solicitor–client communication.

[C]  Yes, irrespective of its purpose.

[D]  Yes, if ordered to do so by the Minister of Health.


**31.** Concerning the Civil Evidence Act 1968, s. 4, which of the following propositions is INCORRECT?

[A]  The section operates without prejudice to s. 5 of that Act.

[B]  The section applies in relation to statements of non-expert opinion as it applies in relation to statements of fact.

[C]  Personal knowledge on the part of the original supplier of the information (from which the record was compiled) may not be inferred by the Court.

[D]  There is no limit to the number of intermediaries through whom the information may have been supplied to the compiler of the record, provided that each such intermediary was acting under a duty.

**32.** In a civil action by Philip against Denis arising out of the collision of 2 ships, both of which sank, aerial photographs taken of the 2 ships after the collision but before they sank have been admitted in evidence. Philip calls Wendy, an expert in the field of maritime accident reconstruction. Wendy gives evidence that she examined the aerial photographs and consulted 2 articles (of which she is not the author) in a technical journal called 'Maritime Accident Reconstruction Monthly'. She also testifies that the journal is a source upon which maritime accident experts generally rely. Lastly she testifies that on the basis of her examination of the photographs, coupled with the information obtained from the articles, 'Denis's ship almost certainly crashed into the side of Philip's ship'. This evidence is:

[A]  Inadmissible, because it is evidence of opinion based in part on facts which are not within Wendy's personal knowledge.

[B]  Inadmissible, because it contains an opinion on the ultimate facts in issue in the case.

[C]  Inadmissible, because Wendy's evidence alone cannot be used to establish that the journal is a source on which experts in this field generally rely.

[D]  Admissible.

**33.** Mrs Militant, a civil servant in the Ministry of Agriculture, was expecting to be promoted but then found that a colleague, Placid, was promoted instead. Mrs Militant suspects that she was passed over because she has been active in AGRO (her trade union) and/or because she is a woman. She is therefore bringing proceedings before an industrial tribunal. She has asked the Ministry to disclose to the tribunal the personal file they have on her, and also that of Placid. The Ministry have refused on the ground that since the files contain information supplied in strict confidence they should not be disclosed in the interests of the proper functioning of the public service. How should the Chairman of the tribunal rule?

[A] That he should inspect the files himself, and order discovery of one or both if he thinks it necessary.

[B] That the grounds stated by the Ministry were right and they must withhold the files.

[C] That the Ministry must disclose to Mrs Militant her own file, but must withhold Placid's.

[D] That the Ministry may disclose or withhold one or both, at their discretion.

**34.** Farmer Dale entered into an agreement with Farmer Hill whereby Hill agreed to graze a flock of Dale's sheep on Hill's farm. Dale's sheep contracted a disease while on Hill's land and had to be destroyed. Dale claims the sheep were negligently kept on boggy land near a river rather than on Hill's drier grazing land. Dale wishes to call 2 local farmers with similar holdings to say that on the basis of their experience sheep should never be grazed on land like the land in question because of the risk of contracting diseases. Both of the proposed witnesses have been sheep farming for over 25 years, but neither has any formal qualifications. Their evidence is:

**[A]** Admissible expert testimony (subject to compliance with advance notice procedures).

**[B]** Inadmissible, because it is opinion evidence on matters requiring expert testimony but the witnesses are not experts.

**[C]** Inadmissible as raising collateral issues as to what other persons have done on occasions other than the one in issue.

**[D]** Admissible as relevant factual, rather than opinion evidence.

**35.** Len was convicted of stealing certain items of jewellery. The jewellery was returned to the alleged owner Oswald. Len then commences a civil action for conversion against Oswald alleging that he (Len) is and always has been the owner of the jewellery. Oswald defends the action and introduces evidence of Len's conviction.

Evidence of Len's conviction:

**[A]** Is inadmissible.

**[B]** Is admissible but only on the issue of credibility.

**[C]** Is conclusive evidence that Len stole the jewellery.

**[D]** Creates a rebuttable presumption that Len stole the jewellery.

**36.** Phillipa is suing Desmond in the High Court. She has served on him a notice in accordance with RSC Ord. 38, r. 21 indicating her desire to give in evidence, for the truth of its contents, a statement made by Finola which is admissible in evidence by virtue of the Civil Evidence Act 1968, s. 2. The notice states, inter alia, that Finola cannot be called as a witness because she is dead. At the trial, Finola's statement is given in evidence. Desmond wishes to adduce evidence that Finola, after making the statement referred to in Phillipa's notice, but before her death, made another statement inconsistent with the earlier statement. Evidence of the inconsistent statement will be:

[A]   Admissible in any event.

[B]   Inadmissible, unless Desmond served a counter-notice.

[C]   Inadmissible, because it was made after and not before the statement referred to in Phillipa's notice.

[D]   Admissible if Desmond served notice of his intent to adduce such evidence or the judge, despite Desmond's failure to serve such notice, decides to admit such evidence as a matter of discretion.


**37.** Six months ago, Beatrice was arrested by PC Clout on a charge of supplying cocaine. At the trial, 3 months ago, she was acquitted. She has now commenced proceedings claiming damages for malicious prosecution. In the course of this civil trial, PC Clout, in his evidence-in-chief, testifies that he arrested Beatrice 'acting on information received in confidence'. In cross-examination, he is asked to name the source of the 'information received'. Should the judge allow PC Clout to answer this question?

[A]   No, because the information was received in confidence.

[B]   No, because it is in the public interest to protect the identity of informants.

[C]   Yes, because disclosure of the name of the informant is necessary for Beatrice to establish her claim.

[D]   Yes, but only if PC Clout is willing to answer it.

**38.** A national newspaper suggests that a new Bishop's appointment has been made on political grounds. The Bishop sues for libel. At the trial, the journalist who wrote the article gives evidence that the Bishop was appointed after making a large donation to the political party in power and after undertaking to support government policy when appointed. When asked to name the sources of his information the journalist refuses, saying that he has a privilege under the Contempt of Court Act 1981, s. 10. How should the judge rule?

[A] He has an absolute right to refuse to disclose his source.

[B] He need not answer unless it is 'necessary' in the interests of justice or national security or for the prevention of disorder or crime.

[C] He must not answer without his source's consent because the public interest requires free access to the media to expose official wrongdoing.

[D] He must answer.

**39.** Charles is suing Daniel for breach of contract. Charles, in the light of a statement made by Edward to his (Charles's) solicitors, calls Edward as a witness. Edward gives evidence which totally contradicts the statement, and the judge allows him to be treated as hostile. The statement is:

[A] Inadmissible hearsay.

[B] Admissible as proof of its contents and to establish Edward's inconsistency.

[C] Admissible *only* to establish Edward's inconsistency.

[D] Inadmissible because irrelevant.

**40.** Which of the following statements about the doctrine of judicial notice after enquiry is INCORRECT?

[A] The doctrine applies only to facts which are beyond serious dispute, notorious or of common knowledge.
[B] The doctrine allows the judge, before taking judicial notice, to consult sources such as authoritative works of reference and almanacs.
[C] Once the judge has taken judicial notice of a fact under the doctrine, then generally it will constitute a binding legal precedent.
[D] Under the doctrine, the rules of evidence do not apply to the enquiry undertaken by the judge.

## CRIMINAL LITIGATION AND SENTENCING

**41.** Robbie, aged 20, pleads guilty at the Yellowbrick Crown Court to a charge of robbery. You mitigate on his behalf and draw to the Court's attention the 'exceptional circumstances' disclosed in his pre-sentence report, namely that he lives with his disabled mother who is considerably reliant upon him. Which one of the following sentences will the Court NOT be able to impose:

[A] A sentence of 2 years' imprisonment suspended for 2 years.
[B] A sentence of 2 years' detention in a young offender institution.
[C] A combination order.
[D] A community service order.

**42.** Martha is charged on indictment with murder. Before arraignment her counsel raises the issue of her fitness to plead. The judge decides that she is unfit to plead and makes a hospital order in respect of her. This procedure is flawed in that:

[A] The issue of fitness to plead should only be raised at the end of the prosecution's case.
[B] The issue of fitness to plead should have been determined by a jury.
[C] A hospital order is not an appropriate response to a finding of unfitness to plead.
[D] The issue of fitness to plead cannot be raised when the charge is murder.

**43.** A jury are unable to reach a verdict and the Judge discharges them. Which one of the following statements is correct?

[A] There must be a re-trial.
[B] There may be a re-trial if the prosecution wish to proceed.
[C] The charge against the defendant is left on the file marked not to be proceeded with unless the Crown Court or the Court of Appeal gives leave.
[D] The defendant is acquitted.

**44.** Nickie, aged 19, appears at the Picklewig Crown Court on committal for sentence from the Picklegown Magistrates' Court on 2 charges of theft from her employer. The judge imposes a sentence of 9 months' detention in a young offender institution in respect of the first charge and a probation order for 12 months in respect of the second. The judge:

[A] Has power to impose these 2 sentences on the same occasion.

[B] Has no power to impose these 2 sentences on the same occasion but it would be unprofessional for counsel to correct the judge in respect of the mistake.

[C] Has power to impose these 2 sentences on the same occasion subject to Nickie's consent.

[D] Has no power to impose the 2 sentences on the same occasion and it would be the professional duty of counsel to draw the judge's attention to the mistake.

**45.** Sheila was committed for trial on a charge of theft of a camera. The committal papers disclosed, among other things, that she was arrested the day after the alleged theft when she tried to sell the camera, for a fraction of its usual price, to a plain clothes policeman. The indictment contains a single count alleging theft. At the end of the prosecution's evidence, the prosecution seek to add a second count alleging handling stolen goods, namely the camera. This application:

[A] Will succeed, unless, having regard to the merits of the case and the possibility of adjourning, the new count cannot be added without injustice to Sheila.

[B] Will fail, because the counts in the indictment must correspond with the charges found by the magistrates on committal for trial.

[C] Will fail, because all applications relating to the form of the indictment must be made on arraignment, and it is now too late.

[D] Is unnecessary because the prosecution have an absolute right to amend the form of an indictment at any time.

**46.** Darren pleads guilty in the Magistrates' Court to theft. He now tells you that the offence was in fact committed by Eric, who bullied him into taking the blame for it, saying that Darren's little boy 'would live to regret it' if he did not. Darren now wishes to appeal to the Crown Court. In this situation:

[A] He has no right to appeal against conviction, but may do so with the leave of the Crown Court, and, if leave is given, the case will be reheard in the Crown Court.

[B] He has no right to appeal against conviction but may challenge the validity of the plea, and, if that challenge is successful, the case will be remitted to the magistrates for rehearing.

[C] He has no right to appeal against conviction, but may do so with the leave of the Magistrates' Court, and if leave is given, the case will be reheard in the Crown Court.

[D] He has the right to appeal against conviction by serving notice on the Magistrates' Court and the magistrates will rehear the case themselves.

**47.** An indictment contains a single count for robbery. The jury purports to return a verdict of 'not guilty of robbery, but guilty of theft'. Such a verdict is:

[A] Valid, because robbery includes by implication an allegation of an offence of theft.

[B] Valid, because theft is a less serious offence than robbery.

[C] Invalid, because sufficient particulars for a count alleging theft cannot be arrived at by deleting particulars from the existing robbery count.

[D] Invalid, because the jury is only empowered to return a verdict in respect of those offences for which the accused has been arraigned.

**48.** Ian is charged with 2 offences: (a) theft of a necklace from Evanhams on 1 January; and (b) living on the earnings of a prostitute throughout the month of February. He is committed to the Crown Court on both offences in separate committal proceedings (the offences are not connected). His defence in (a) is that at the time of the theft he was at home, alone, suffering from flu, and in (b) during the third week in February he was in France on business and not staying at the prostitute's flat as alleged by the prosecution. In these circumstances, which one of the following statements is correct?

[A]  An alibi notice must be given in both cases.
[B]  An alibi notice is not required in either case.
[C]  An alibi notice is required in case (a) but not in case (b).
[D]  An alibi notice is required in case (b) but not in case (a).


**49.**  Randy, aged 16, appears in the Toughbench Youth Court and pleads guilty to 4 charges of indecent assault on women. The offences are triable either way and the maximum sentence for each offence is 10 years. Which one of the following statements about the magistrates' powers is correct?

When sentencing, the magistrates may:

[A]  Impose a maximum custodial sentence of 12 months in aggregate for the offences.
[B]  Impose a maximum custodial sentence of 6 months in aggregate for the offences.
[C]  Commit him to the Crown Court for sentence where he may be sentenced to a maximum custodial sentence of 6 months per offence to run consecutively, amounting to 2 years in aggregate.
[D]  Commit him to the Crown Court for sentence where he may be sentenced to a maximum custodial sentence of 10 years per offence to run concurrently, amounting to 10 years in aggregate.

**50.** At the end of the prosecution case, counsel for the defence makes a submission of no case to answer. The Judge rejects this submission and orders the trial to continue. The alleged defect in the prosecution case is rectified by cross-examination of the defence witnesses. The defendant is convicted, and appeals solely on the basis that the Judge was wrong to reject the submission.

Assuming that the Judge was wrong in law to reject the submission, which of the following actions is the Court of Appeal most likely to take?

[A] Quash the conviction, because, had the Judge not erred, the defendant would have been acquitted.

[B] Quash the conviction, and order a *venire de novo*.

[C] Apply the proviso, and uphold the conviction if satisfied that no substantial miscarriage of justice actually occurred.

[D] Examine the evidence given during both the prosecution and defence cases, and decide the appeal on that basis.

**51.** John is charged with indecent assault upon Tracey. It is alleged that the assault took place in one of the cubicles at the physiotherapy department of the hospital where John works as a porter. The only prosecution evidence is that of Tracey and her mother (who says that Tracey returned home in a distressed state on the day in question). After the jury have retired, they send a note to the Judge asking for further evidence, namely whether or not the adjacent cubicles were in use at the time of the alleged assault so that any protests by Tracey might have been heard. As counsel in the case, you are asked by the Judge whether he can comply with this request. What should you say to him?

[A]  The jury are only entitled to hear additional evidence if the Judge first gives leave to the prosecution to re-open their case.

[B]  The jury are entitled to ask for any additional evidence provided that the evidence is given in open Court, in the presence of the accused and of both counsel.

[C]  The jury are not entitled to ask any questions once they have retired.

[D]  The jury are not entitled to hear additional evidence after they have retired.

**52.** Stan has been remanded in custody by Exchester Magistrates' Court following a fully argued bail application. He wishes to challenge the refusal of bail. Which one of the following statements is correct?

[A]  If Stan applies to the Crown Court and the Judge refuses bail, Stan can only apply to the High Court with leave of the Crown Court Judge or of a High Court Judge.

[B]  If Stan applies to the High Court and the Judge refuses bail, Stan cannot then apply to the Crown Court.

[C]  Stan may apply to either the High Court or the Crown Court and then, if unsuccessful, to the other one but should inform the second Court of the unsuccessful application.

[D]  The High Court only has jurisdiction if the grounds for obtaining a writ of habeas corpus are satisfied.

**53.** Bill, aged 18, appears at the Carhot Magistrates' Court and is convicted of aggravated motor vehicle taking which was alleged to have occurred on 27 March 1994 in Carhot Green. He has 3 previous findings of guilt for taking motor vehicles without consent for which he received an Attendance Centre Order, a Supervision Order and a Community Service Order respectively. The offence is very prevalent in the Carhot area. When sentencing, the Carhot magistrates should NOT have regard to one of the following considerations. Which one?

[A] The need to impose an 'exemplary' sentence to serve as an example to other young offenders.
[B] The prevalence of the offence in that area.
[C] The offender's previous offences and any failure to respond to previous sentences.
[D] The need to impose a sentence which is commensurate with the seriousness of the offence.

**54.** Daniel is charged with burglary contrary to s. 9(1)(b) of the Theft Act 1968 at Pencaster Crown Court, in that he entered a building as a trespasser and stole a lawnmower. The evidence, from both the prosecution and the defence, shows that he had had permission both to enter the building and to borrow the lawnmower, but that he had failed to return it when he should because he had decided to keep it permanently. Daniel is convicted and now appeals to the Court of Appeal. The Court of Appeal accepts that he did not enter as a trespasser, and that he had permission to borrow the lawnmower, but holds that he had wrongfully retained it and did not intend to return it to its owner. In these circumstances, which of the following courses of action is the Court of Appeal most likely to adopt?

[A] It will quash the conviction.
[B] It will uphold the conviction.
[C] It will quash the conviction, but substitute a conviction for theft.
[D] It will quash the conviction and order a re-trial.

**55.** Albert is convicted of a series of thefts and related offences (some summary and some triable either way) at the Newtown Magistrates' Court. The magistrates now consider that the combination of offences is so serious that greater punishment should be inflicted than they have power to impose. In these circumstances the magistrates:

[A]   Have no choice but to sentence him themselves.
[B]   May commit the triable either way offences to the Crown Court for sentence, but may not commit the summary offences.
[C]   May commit the triable either way offences to the Crown Court for sentence, but must adjourn the summary offences *sine die.*
[D]   May commit all the offences to the Crown Court for sentence.


**56.** If a jury which has been given a majority verdict direction is still unable to reach a verdict, the Judge may give them further directions. These further directions must NOT include one of the following elements. Which one?

[A]   That the jurors have a duty to act not only as individuals but also collectively.
[B]   That jurors should be willing to give and take.
[C]   That jurors should be prepared to alter their views if they can do so and still remain consistent to the oath which they have taken.
[D]   That jurors should bear in mind the inconvenience of a fresh trial if they cannot reach a verdict.

**57.** Alan was committed for trial on a charge of blackmail. The committal papers also indicated that Alan had perpetrated an offence of theft (which was wholly unconnected with the alleged blackmail); however Alan was not committed on any charge of theft. The prosecution preferred two indictments – one containing the count of blackmail, the other a count of theft. At the trial of the blackmail indictment Alan was acquitted. At the trial of the theft indictment an application by Alan's counsel to have the indictment quashed was rejected by the trial judge.

The trial judge's decision was

[A] Incorrect because the prosecution can never prefer an indictment which charges an offence on which there was no committal.

[B] Incorrect because the prosecution can only prefer an indictment which charges an offence on which there was no committal if the offence in question could properly be joined (in the same indictment) with the offence(s) on which there was a committal.

[C] Correct because the prosecution can always prefer an indictment in respect of any offence which is disclosed by the committal papers (whether or not there has been a committal on that charge).

[D] Correct because the prosecution can prefer an indictment in respect of any offence which falls within the same Statute as an offence for which an accused has been committed.

**58.** On 16 April 1992 Peter is placed on probation for two years by Grimchester Crown Court for an offence of theft. In July 1994 he appears before the Doomchester Crown Court and pleads guilty to an offence of obtaining property by deception, this offence having been committed on 1 April 1994. The following statements relate to the powers of Doomchester Crown Court to deal with the offence of theft from 1992. Only one of these statements is correct. Which one?

[A] No action can be taken in respect of the theft as the date of the conviction for the later offence is more than 2 years after the date on which the probation order was made.

[B] Doomchester Crown Court can re-sentence in respect of the theft but only with the consent of Grimchester Crown Court.

[C] Doomchester Crown Court can re-sentence in respect of the theft but can only pass a non-custodial sentence for the theft.

[D] Doomchester Crown Court can re-sentence in respect of the theft and can pass a custodial or non-custodial sentence for the theft.

**59.** Where the Court of Appeal considers the making of an order for loss of time spent in custody pending an appeal, and assuming that the Court adopts the approach set out in the 1980 *Practice Direction* on loss of time, which one of the following statements is correct?

[A] The order is unlikely to be made when leave to appeal is refused by the single judge of the Court of Appeal, if grounds of appeal are settled by counsel and supported by his written opinion.

[B] The order is unlikely to be made where leave to appeal is refused by the full Court of Appeal, if grounds of appeal are settled by counsel and supported by his written opinion.

[C] Both [A] and [B] are correct.

[D] Neither [A] nor [B] is correct.

**60.** Arnold, aged 20, is sentenced to 2 years' imprisonment by a Crown Court judge. He wishes to appeal against this sentence. In these circumstances, which one of the following statements is correct?

[A] Arnold does not need leave to appeal, because the sentence is wrong in law.

[B] Arnold needs to get leave to appeal from the single judge of the Court of Appeal, because the appeal is against sentence.

[C] Arnold needs to get leave to appeal but, as the sentence is wrong in law, such leave may be obtained from the Registrar of Criminal Appeals.

[D] The trial judge cannot certify that the case is fit for appeal, because it is an appeal against sentence only and not against conviction.

## CRIMINAL EVIDENCE

**61.** David is a porter at a large office block. He is required to keep a detailed log of all visitors, and any incidents that may occur. One day, Francis visited the block, asking to see George, who works in the block. George met Francis in the entrance hall. A fight broke out and George was injured. Shortly afterwards, David made an entry in his log-book recording the incident. Francis has now been charged with causing George grievous bodily harm. By the date of the trial, David has no recollection of the incident at all. The entry in David's log-book is:

[A] Inadmissible hearsay.

[B] Admissible, in principle, under the Criminal Justice Act 1988, s. 24.

[C] Admissible, in principle, under the Criminal Justice Act 1988, s. 23.

[D] Admissible as original evidence.

**62.** Amanda is charged with blackmail. Police officers claim that when they called at Amanda's house on a totally unrelated matter (routine door-to-door enquiries about a missing child), Amanda, on seeing them, had said: 'It's about the blackmail isn't it? I'm sorry. I knew you'd catch me sooner or later.' Amanda admits that the officers called and asked about a missing child, but categorically denies that she ever made the alleged confession: she alleges that the officers have invented the confession (but does not allege any other improper behaviour on their part). The prosecution intend to call the police officers to prove Amanda's confession. Such evidence is:

[A]  Admissible, but only if the judge holds a voir dire and gives a ruling to this effect.
[B]  Inadmissible, because Amanda categorically denies making the confession.
[C]  Admissible without recourse to a voir dire.
[D]  Inadmissible hearsay.


**63.** Sam is charged with murdering his wife, Tina, by stabbing her with a knife. The prosecution case is that the reason for the offence was the discovery by Sam that Tina was having an adulterous affair with his best friend, Victor. According to Sam, however, he made no such discovery. The day before the alleged murder, Tina wrote a letter to Vera, a friend, stating: 'Yesterday, Sam discovered me and Victor in bed together!' The contents of this letter are:

[A]  Inadmissible hearsay.
[B]  Admissible under the Criminal Justice Act 1988, s. 24, subject to the discretion to exclude under s. 25.
[C]  Admissible as a dying declaration.
[D]  Admissible under the Criminal Justice Act 1988, s. 23, subject to the discretion to exclude under s. 25.

**64.** Plain clothes police officers, without announcing that they were police officers, entered 'Eric's Minimarket' and bought some whisky. As a result of this purchase, Eric was subsequently charged with selling liquor without a licence. At the trial, counsel for Eric submits that evidence of the purchase should be excluded under the Police and Criminal Evidence Act 1984, s. 78. What should the Court do?

[A] Admit the evidence, because to do so has no adverse effect on the fairness of the proceedings.
[B] Admit the evidence, because the circumstances in which it was obtained are irrelevant.
[C] Exclude the evidence, because of the officers' trickery.
[D] Exclude the evidence, because before purchasing the whisky, the officers should have administered a caution.

**65.** Anthony is charged with theft. Shortly after his arrest he made a full confession to the charge. At the trial evidence is given by his girlfriend, Beatrice, that she had seen him during his detention for questioning and had told him that if he confessed he would get bail. His counsel submits that the confession should be excluded under the Police and Criminal Evidence Act 1984, s. 76(2)(b) (likelihood of unreliability). The trial judge finds that Beatrice probably did make the statement about bail but nevertheless rules that the confession is admissible. This ruling could have been correct on only one of the following grounds. Which one?

[A] Under s. 76, a confession is always admissible if obtained by someone other than a person in authority.
[B] The judge was satisfied that Anthony's confession was true.
[C] The judge was satisfied that Anthony's confession was not obtained in consequence of Beatrice's statement.
[D] There is an overriding discretion to ignore the effect of s. 76(2)(b) and include confession statements.

**66.** Michael, aged 20, is tried on indictment for indecent assault. The prosecution case depends substantially on a confession he made to 2 police officers who interviewed him after his arrest. No other person was present at the interview. The trial judge on a voir dire relating to the admissibility of this confession concludes that Michael is 'mentally handicapped' (as defined in the Police and Criminal Evidence Act 1984). Which of the following statements about this case is *correct*?

[A] The judge, having concluded that Michael is mentally handicapped, is required by law to exclude Michael's confession.

[B] If the judge admits Michael's confession, she is required by law to warn the jury that there is a special need for caution before convicting the accused in reliance on the confession.

[C] Having regard to his mental handicap, Michael is eligible to give unsworn evidence.

[D] Michael is eligible to give sworn evidence but only if he satisfies the judge that he understands the divine sanction of the oath.

**67.** Peter and Rupert were charged with an armed bank robbery. Photographs which had been taken by a security camera automatically at 5-second intervals during the course of the raid, were produced at the trial. No witnesses were called as to identification, and the jury were invited to look at the photographs, look at the defendants in the dock and conclude, if they thought it right to do so, that the men in the photographs were in fact the men in the dock. Peter and Rupert were convicted, and appeal on the ground that the photographs were improperly admitted. The appeal is likely to:

[A] Succeed, because admission of the photographs was in breach of the hearsay rule.

[B] Fail, because the photographs were admissible under the Criminal Justice Act 1988, s. 24.

[C] Succeed, because the admission of the photographs was in breach of the rule against previous consistent statements.

[D] Fail, because photographs are in a class of their own to which neither the rule against hearsay nor the rule against previous consistent statements applies.


**68.** Rob is charged with murdering Susan. Tom, an associate of Rob, signs a death-bed statement to the effect that he, not Rob, murdered Susan. Tom dies before Rob's trial. Subject to any discretion that the judge may have to exclude it, Tom's statement is admissible:

[A] Under the Police and Criminal Evidence Act 1984, s. 76 as a confession.

[B] Under the Criminal Justice Act 1988, s. 23.

[C] As part of the *res gestae.*

[D] As a dying declaration.

**69.** Robin is charged with handling a stolen video recorder. His defence is that he purchased it, without knowledge or belief that it was stolen, from a former colleague who has since emigrated. He claims that the colleague had said to him at the time of the purchase 'I bought it from a shop last Christmas, though I haven't kept the receipt or guarantee.' At trial, evidence of what the colleague allegedly said to him will be admissible, for the defence, as:

[A] Part of the *res gestae*.
[B] Evidence of Robin's lack of knowledge or belief that the goods were stolen.
[C] Evidence that the goods were not stolen.
[D] Hearsay evidence under s. 23 of the Criminal Justice Act 1988.


**70.** Whenever a trial judge directs the jury on the proper use of lies by the accused to support evidence of guilt, the direction should make it clear to the jury that they should be satisfied on all the following matters except one. Which one?

[A] That the lie was deliberate.
[B] That the lie was in writing' or otherwise recorded in documentary form.
[C] That there was no innocent motive for the lie.
[D] That the lie relates to a material issue.

**71.** Joan is charged with theft. At her trial she challenges under the Police and Criminal Evidence Act 1984, s. 76(2)(b) (likelihood of unreliability) the admissibility of a confession she made to the police. The judge rules that the confession is admissible holding that (1) s. 76(2)(b) requires some element of improper conduct on the part of the interrogator (which is absent in Joan's case); and (2) the test is whether the confession Joan actually made was obtained in consequence of anything said or done which was likely, in the circumstances existing at the time, to render unreliable 'any confession which might be made by her in consequence thereof'. This ruling is:

[A] Correct on the first point, wrong on the second.
[B] Correct on both points.
[C] Incorrect on the first point, correct on the second.
[D] Incorrect on both points.

**72.** John is suspected of committing a series of burglaries. The police arrested him and detained him for questioning. He made a full confession and was charged with the burglaries. At his trial, he challenges the admissibility of the confession, representing that it was obtained by oppression. The trial judge makes two rulings: (1) that she will only hold a voir dire if the defence adduce some evidence in support of their representation; and (2) that if such a voir dire does take place, she will be entitled to enquire into the truth or falsity of the confession. This ruling is:

[A] Wrong on both points.
[B] Correct on both points.
[C] Wrong on the first point, correct on the second.
[D] Correct on the first point, wrong on the second.

**73.** Jim was overtaken by a yellow Ford Escort car and made a mental note of the registration number, XYZ 1. Moments later the Escort pulled out to overtake on the brow of a hill and an oncoming car driven by Ken was forced to swerve off the road and into a ditch. Jim stopped and told a police officer, Luke, what he had seen, including the registration number of the Ford Escort. Luke made a written note of Jim's statement (but this was not read back to Jim nor signed by Jim). The Ford Escort is traced to Adam who is charged with dangerous driving. Jim has since died. Luke's note is:

[A] Inadmissible hearsay.

[B] Admissible, in principle, under the Criminal Justice Act 1988, s. 23.

[C] Admissible, in principle, under the Criminal Justice Act 1988, s. 24.

[D] Admissible as a declaration in the course of duty by a person deceased at the time of trial.


**74.** Same facts as in Question 73 above, except that Jim told Ken (the driver of the car which was forced into the ditch) what he had seen and Ken relayed Jim's statement to Luke who wrote it down. Luke's note is:

[A] Inadmissible hearsay.

[B] Admissible under the Criminal Justice Act 1988, s. 23 (subject to the discretion to exclude under s. 25 and/ or the requirement of leave under s. 26).

[C] Admissible under the Criminal Justice Act 1988, s. 24 (subject to the discretion to exclude under s. 25 and/ or the requirement of leave under s. 26).

[D] Admissible under the public records exception.

**75.** Bill is charged with theft. The case against him depends substantially on the correctness of a visual identification of him by Clare, which Bill alleges to be mistaken. At the trial, the judge comes to the conclusion that the quality of Clare's identification evidence is poor. What should he do?

[A] Direct an acquittal, whatever the nature of the other evidence in the case.

[B] Direct an acquittal, unless there is other evidence, which must be corroboration in the strict sense, which goes to support the correctness of the identification evidence.

[C] Direct an acquittal, unless there is other evidence, whether or not corroboration in the strict sense, which goes to support the correctness of the identification evidence.

[D] As in [C], but subject to the proviso that if there is supportive evidence, he must direct the jury that if he had thought there was insufficient identification evidence, he would have directed them to acquit.

**76.** Victor and Walter are charged with handling stolen goods, namely machine tools which, the prosecution allege, were stolen from XYZ (Machine Tools) Ltd. On being questioned by the police, Victor and Walter admit that the goods must have originally come from XYZ (Machine Tools) Ltd, because they saw the labels attached to the boxes in which they were originally packed, which read: 'XYZ ( Machine Tools) Ltd. Do not remove.' However, they also say that they bought the tools from a man they had arranged to meet in a pub, having seen an advert in the local paper that tools were for sale and having rung the number given. At the trial, the prosecution seek to establish that the goods were stolen from XYZ (Machine Tools) Ltd by relying on Victor's and Walter's admission as to their origin. As to whether the goods were stolen from XYZ (Machine Tools) Ltd, these admissions are:

[A]   Inadmissible as they were based solely on the reading of the labels and have no more evidential value than the labels themselves.

[B]   Admissible, not being hearsay, because the Court is not concerned with the truth of the statements but with whether the statements were made.

[C]   Admissible as admissions which, in the circumstances, are at least prima facie evidence that the goods were stolen.

[D]   Admissible in law, but open to exclusion under s. 78 of the Police and Criminal Evidence Act 1984.

**77.** Dick and his wife Emily were jointly indicted, Dick being charged with the supply of cocaine, and Emily with its importation. Counsel for Dick made a successful application for 2 separate trials, and the trial continued against Dick alone. (Emily's trial will take place in 3 months' time.) In the course of Dick's trial, counsel for the prosecution asks Dick, in cross-examination, to explain how he came to be in possession of the cocaine. Dick refuses to answer and, in the absence of the jury, explains to the judge that to do so would incriminate his spouse. How should the judge rule?

[A] Dick may answer the question if he wishes, the choice being entirely his.
[B] Dick may answer the question, but only with the consent of his wife.
[C] Dick may answer the question, but only with the consent of both his wife and her legal advisers.
[D] Dick must answer the question.

**78**. Michael is charged with assaulting Paul, a fellow employee. In his defence, Michael claims that he was acting in reasonable self defence (although Michael accepts that Paul had only lightly tapped him on the arm). Michael says in evidence that his mother died shortly before the alleged assault and he was feeling particularly sensitive at the time. He wishes to call a psychiatrist to give evidence that shortly after the alleged offence he, Michael, appeared to be a person suffering from severe sorrow following a recent bereavement; that he was likely to overreact to any adverse circumstances; but was not suffering from any mental illness. Will the psychiatrist's evidence be admissible?

[A] Yes, because it is the evidence of a qualified medical practitioner in his field of competence and is relevant to Michael's defence.

[B] Yes, but only in order to confirm the credibility of Michael's testimony as to his state of mind.

[C] No, because it is a self-serving statement in that the psychiatrist is simply repeating what Michael told him after the event.

[D] No, because the tribunal of fact does not need expert assistance in assessing Michael's alleged mental condition at the relevant time.

**79.** Marie was suspected by Naomi, a store detective, of shoplifting. She was detained and questioned about her suspected commission of the offence by Naomi and (according to Naomi) eventually admitted that she was shoplifting. At Marie's trial her counsel wishes to argue that her confession should be excluded under the Police and Criminal Evidence Act 1984, s. 78 because Naomi had interviewed Marie without complying with the Code of Practice for interviews made pursuant to s. 66 of that Act (Code C). Would such a course be justified?

[A]   No, because Naomi's questioning of Marie did not amount to an interview for the purposes of Code C.
[B]   Yes, because on the facts the judge *could* conclude that Naomi was bound to comply with Code C.
[C]   No, because only the police are bound to comply with Code C.
[D]   Yes, because anyone who questions a suspect must comply with Code C.


**80.** Dugan is charged with criminal damage following a demonstration outside the civic centre. An eye-witness told PC Bloggs that the man who had thrown a brick at the window had run into the building on the other side of the square. PC Bloggs found Dugan alone in the building and arrested him. The eye-witness cannot be traced. Can PC Bloggs give evidence at the trial of what the eye-witness told him?

[A]   Yes, because it merely explains PC Bloggs's actions.
[B]   Yes, because it is circumstantial evidence that Dugan committed the offence.
[C]   No, because it is inadmissible hearsay.
[D]   No, because it is irrelevant to the facts in issue.

# APPENDIX 1

# ANSWERS TO MCT – PART 1

| CIVIL LITIGATION | CIVIL EVIDENCE | CRIMINAL LITIGATION | CRIMINAL EVIDENCE |
|---|---|---|---|
| 1. B | 18. B | 31. B | 46. A |
| 2. C | 19. B | 32. C | 47. B |
| 3. A | 20. C | 33. B | 48. B |
| 4. C | 21. D | 34. C | 49. D |
| 5. D | 22. C | 35. D | 50. C |
| 6. B | 23. C | 36. D | 51. C |
| 7. D | 24. B | 37. A | 52. C |
| 8. B | 25. A | 38. D | 53. D |
| 9. A | 26. C | 39. A | 54. D |
| 10. A | 27. C | 40. D | 55. D |
| 11. D | 28. B | 41. A | 56. C |
| 12. C | 29. D | 42. B | 57. C |
| 13. B | 30. A | 43. C | 58. B |
| 14. C | | 44. B | 59. C |
| 15. D | | 45. C | 60. B |
| 16. A | | | |
| 17. C | | | |

# APPENDIX 2

# ANSWERS TO MCT – PART 2

| CIVIL LITIGATION | CIVIL EVIDENCE | CRIMINAL LITIGATION AND SENTENCING | CRIMINAL EVIDENCE |
|---|---|---|---|
| 1. A | 24. B | 41. A | 61. B |
| 2. D | 25. D | 42. B | 62. C |
| 3. C | 26. B | 43. B | 63. D |
| 4. C | 27. B | 44. D | 64. A |
| 5. B | 28. C | 45. A | 65. C |
| 6. B | 29. B | 46. B | 66. B |
| 7. A | 30. A | 47. A | 67. D |
| 8. B | 31. C | 48. C | 68. B |
| 9. D | 32. D | 49. A | 69. B |
| 10. D | 33. A | 50. A | 70. B |
| 11. B | 34. A | 51. D | 71. C |
| 12. A | 35. D | 52. C | 72. A |
| 13. B | 36. D | 53. A | 73. C |
| 14. A | 37. B | 54. C | 74. A |
| 15. C | 38. B | 55. D | 75. C |
| 16. B | 39. B | 56. D | 76. A |
| 17. D | 40. A | 57. B | 77. D |
| 18. B | | 58. A | 78. D |
| 19. C | | 59. A | 79. B |
| 20. D | | 60. B | 80. C |
| 21. A | | | |
| 22. D | | | |
| 23. A | | | |

# APPENDIX 3

# NOTE-FORM ANSWERS TO MCT – PART 1

## CIVIL LITIGATION

**1.** The first one or two questions in the Civil Litigation MCT are intended to be relatively straightforward. When this question has appeared in the tests it has presented few problems. Article 5 of the High Court and County Court Jurisdiction Order 1991 requires actions for damages in respect of personal injuries to be commenced in a County Court where the plaintiff does not reasonably expect to recover more than £50,000. Mavis has minimal special damages, and her claim for general damages for pain, suffering and loss of amenity, although not small, is clearly worth a great deal less than £50,000 (answer [B]). The few candidates who went wrong tended to choose answer [A], apparently forgetting that claims with a value exceeding £50,000 can be commenced in the High Court.

**2.** Again, this is intended to be a straightforward question (but a little more difficult than question 1), and has been deliberately placed at the beginning of the test. In order to answer this question it is necessary to have learnt the basic conditions that must be established before the Court will consider granting an *Anton Piller* order. These were laid down by Ormrod LJ in *Anton Piller KG* v *Manufacturing Processes Ltd* [1976] Ch 55, and can be found in the *Civil Litigation*

*Manual* at 14.4. The question asks you to identify the incorrect condition, which is answer [C]. This answer is, to some extent, disguised by the fact that *Anton Piller* orders are in practice most commonly applied for in intellectual property cases, but there is no formal condition restricting the making of these orders to such cases.

**3**.  Generally, when a defendant fails to acknowledge service (stating an intention to defend) within 14 days after service (or the deemed date of service if, e.g., service is effected by first-class post) of a writ the plaintiff will think about entering judgment in default. Under RSC Ord. 13 there is a distinction between actions claiming only common law remedies (debt; damages; recovery of goods and possession of land) on the one hand, and actions claiming equitable remedies on the other (see the *Civil Litigation Manual*, 8.2.3 to 8.2.10). As Julia is seeking specific performance (which is the only relief claimed, so there is no question of abandoning the equitable relief in order to enter judgment in default under Ord. 13 for any common law relief claimed) her action is outside the scope of entering judgment under Ord. 13, so the correct answer is [A]. Julia must therefore treat Rick as having acknowledged service. She has served a generally indorsed writ, so she should now serve her Statement of Claim, and can then consider entering judgment in default of pleadings under RSC Ord. 19 if Rick fails to serve a Defence. Answer [B] is nonsense; it is quite permissible to commence an action such as this one by writ, see the *Civil Litigation Manual*, 3.1.2.

**4**.  This question concerns the interrelation between third party proceedings and the main action between the plaintiff and the defendant. As shown by *Stott* v *West Yorkshire Road Car Co. Ltd* [1972] 2 QB 651, in many ways proceedings under a Third Party Notice have a life independent of the main action. However, it is important to distinguish:

(a)    third party claims seeking a contribution or indemnity; and
(b)    third party claims for substantially similar relief or for the resolution of related questions.

Contribution and indemnity claims brought by way of third party notice are obviously dependent on the outcome of the claim by the plaintiff against the defendant. If the plaintiff loses against the defendant, there is nothing for the third party to contribute towards or indemnify the defendant. Therefore, if the plaintiff's action does not proceed to trial, such as where it is dismissed or struck out in the interlocutory stages, and the third party notice only claims a contribution or an indemnity, there is no reason for the third party claim to proceed to trial, and it will fall with the plaintiff's action. However, third party claims in category (b) above go beyond reimbursing the defendant for any liability the defendant may have to the plaintiff, so will continue to trial (if need be) despite the plaintiff's action being e.g. dismissed. In the question Eric has 2 third party claims against George, one in category (a) (the indemnity) and one in category (b) (the damages claim). Hence the correct answer is [C].

**5.** This question concerns the question of bringing proceedings against a defendant outside the jurisdiction. The proposed defendant is domiciled in France (for which see *Civil Litigation Manual*, 9.3.4, a Contracting State to the Brussels Convention, see 9.3.2), so proceedings should normally be commenced in France by virtue of Article 2 (see 9.3.3). The fact the damage was suffered by Marine Fish Ltd in England gives it the alternative of suing in England by virtue of Article 5(3) (see 9.3.6.3). If it chooses to sue in England, proceedings may be commenced without leave (see 9.3.5). Hence the correct answer is [D]. Notice the use of the word 'must' in answers [A] and [B]. There is no need to seek leave under RSC Ord. 11, answer [C].

**6.** Applications for interlocutory injunctions in defamation actions are in an exceptional category and are not governed by the *American Cyanamid* principles where the defendant intends to plead, for example, justification (see *Civil Litigation Manual*, 12.3.2.2). Answer [A] is wrong because it outlines the *American Cyanamid* principles. Answer [D] identifies the wrong exceptional category. Answers [B] and [C] both point to the reason (protection of free speech) and the effect of the rule in defamation cases, the difference between them being as to whether the defendant's assertion of an intention to justify can be challenged. As made clear at 12.3.2.2, an injunction may be granted despite the defendant's protestations if the alleged libel is obviously untrue, so the correct answer is [B].

**7.** Robert's problem is that he would like to sue the persons responsible for ramming his boat, but he does not know who they are. He believes that Vincent, who is a local person and who was apparently present when his boat was hit, will know who was responsible. Pre-action discovery (answer [A]) is only available against a likely defendant, so is not available against Vincent as Robert has no cause of action against him. However, a *Norwich Pharmacal* order can be made against such a person for the purpose of obtaining full information as to the identity of the wrongdoer provided the witness got 'mixed up' in the wrongdoing so as to facilitate its commission. The other boat rammed Robert's boat without any help from Vincent, who was merely painting the harbour. Vincent is therefore a mere witness, and the correct answer is [D]. There is no question of self-incrimination on the facts.

**8.** This question involves the interrelation of two principles in the context of applications for summary judgment. As a result many students find it quite difficult. If Peter, the landlord, had sued David, the tenant, simply for the arrears of rent, David would have had a set-off by virtue of his counterclaim for damages for breach of covenant in the lease, see *British Anzani (Felixstowe) Ltd* v *International Marine Management (UK) Ltd* [1980] QB 137 (*Civil Litigation Manual*, 10.6.4.4). As the rent arrears are £6,000 and the set-off is worth £4,000, David has no defence for the balance (£2,000), so the District Judge would have entered judgment for Peter in the sum of £2,000 and given David unconditional leave to defend for the remainder, answer [C]. However, David has given Peter a cheque for £6,000 and dishonoured it. Peter has wisely chosen to sue on the cheque, not for the rent. Under the so-called cheque rule the Court will disregard defences and set-offs in relation to the underlying transaction, will enter judgment for the full amount of the dishonoured cheque, and will not even grant a stay of execution (see 10.6.4.5). None of the limited defences to cheque actions listed at 10.6.4.5 applies on the facts of this case, so the District Judge will enter judgment for £6,000, answer [B].

**9.** In order to answer this question correctly you need to have sufficient knowledge of the special discovery rules in the Supreme Court Act 1981 to be able to identify the correct type of application to make, and you also need to know about the procedure on making such applications. Isaac is suing Highbury: he has no cause of action against the DSS, who hold the documents he wants to see. Being a non-party, it is not possible to seek an order for pre-action discovery under the Supreme Court Act 1981, s. 33(2) (or its County Court equivalent, the County Courts Act 1984, s. 52(2)). Answer [C] is therefore wrong. An order for discovery against a non-party may be made after proceedings have been commenced against the defendant (here Highbury) under the Supreme Court Act 1981, s. 34(2) (or the County Courts Act 1984, s. 53), provided the action is one in respect of personal injuries or death. Isaac has contracted a respiratory disease. The statutory definition of 'personal injuries' includes disease (see *Civil Litigation Manual*, 17.3.2.1) so answer [D] is wrong. The difference between [A] and [B] turns on whether the application is made by originating summons or interlocutory summons. The Rules of Court specify the latter, so the correct answer is [A]. This also accords with general principles, as the application is being made in pending proceedings between Isaac and Highbury, see RSC Ord. 5, r. 3, set out in the *Civil Litigation Manual* at 3.1.2.

**10.** This question is about the range of orders available to the Court where the other side fails to give full discovery. The Court may order a further and better list of documents (see *Civil Litigation Manual*, 15.7.5), answer [B]; it may order the list of documents to be verified by affidavit (15.7.2), answer [C]; and it may make an order for particular (also known as specific) discovery (15.7.4), answer [D]. The question asks for the incorrect answer, which is [A].

**11.** This is quite a straightforward question on directions. Automatic directions apply in the High Court only to personal injuries cases (but do not apply to claims for personal injuries in Admiralty actions or to medical negligence claims: RSC Ord. 25, r. 8(5)). Yasmin's action against her employer is an ordinary personal injuries action, so the correct answer is [D]. See *Civil Litigation Manual*, 16.6.1.

**12**. Is easy to go wrong on this question by not reading it carefully enough. You are asked to identify the proposition that 'best' describes the relevance of the fact the building work has not yet commenced. There are elements of truth in all the answers. Careful reading and a sound understanding of the *American Cyanamid* principles will show that one answer is clearly better than the others. The state of the building work is clearly part of the factual background, but, as will be seen from what follows, it *does* have further relevance to the issues to be considered by the Court, so answer [A] is wrong. The Court has to consider what the plaintiff is seeking to injunct and the likely effects on the parties of the defendant's conduct/the proposed order in deciding whether damages will be an adequate remedy, but this is not 'the only relevance' of the fact in question. Answer [B] is therefore an incomplete answer. There is a similar problem with answer [D]. As the work has not started the injunction will be prohibitory. If the work had been completed the injunction would have compelled Lynn to demolish the building, and would have been mandatory. (Different principles apply depending on whether the proposed injunction is prohibitory or mandatory.) Answer [C] is not worded in a restrictive way, unlike answers [A], [B] and [D]. In *American Cyanamid*, Lord Diplock said that where other factors are evenly balanced, it is a counsel of prudence to seek to preserve the status quo (see *Civil Litigation Manual*, 12.3.1.6), and hence [C] is the best answer.

**13**. This is a procedural point in relations to actions commenced by originating summons. Nevertheless, each time it has appeared in previous MCTs many students have got it wrong. The correct answer is [B], see *Civil Litigation Manual*, 4.5.

**14**. It is first necessary to identify that this question is about applications for interim payments ('a payment on account of any damages Anthony may be entitled to'). On such an application, unless the defendant has admitted liability or the plaintiff has obtained judgment for damages to be assessed, the plaintiff must satisfy the Court he 'would obtain judgment for substantial damages': RSC Ord. 29, r. 11(1)(c), *Civil Litigation Manual*, 11.2.2.1. This narrows the choice down to answers [C] and [D]. The difference between these answers relates to the standard of proof, and it has been held by the Court of Appeal that the civil standard applies (see 11.2.4), but at the higher end of the range, so the answer is [C]. This question illustrates the fact that evidential and procedural rules often overlap.

**15**. This is another question which covers more than one area. The most important thing to get right is the rule on joinder of causes of action. It appears to cover the question of when one should issue a default or fixed date summons (see *Civil Litigation Manual*, 2.2.1 and 2.2.3) and consolidation (see 5.5), but these are largely smoke-screens. Causes of action may be joined in one set of proceedings without leave provided the parties appear in respect of each cause of action in the same legal capacity, see 5.3.1. David and Timothy appear in the same capacities in both the nuisance claim seeking the injunction and the assault claim seeking damages. Neither party is involved in other legal capacity, such as by being a corporation sole or an executor. So a single action can be commenced in respect of both causes of action. Given the connection between the two causes of action, the most practical advice is to commence a single action. As there is a claim for non-monetary relief (the injunction), the proceedings in the County Court must be commenced by a fixed date summons. Hence the correct answer is [D].

**16**. Normally, 'judgment in default' is entered when a defendant fails to acknowledge service at all within the 14 days allowed after service. However, the full phrase is 'judgment in default of notice of intention to defend', which makes clear the alternative basis of entering judgment under RSC Ord. 13, namely that the defendant has acknowledged service, but indicated no intention to defend by ticking the 'no' box to question 2 on the form. This is what has happened here, and Sara can enter judgment straightaway, without waiting for the full 14 days to elapse after service (answer [A]). Sara's claim is for the common law remedy of damages, so there is no need to serve a Statement of Claim, as is the case where the defendant fails to acknowledge service in an action where the plaintiff is seeking equitable relief.

**17.** As with question 14, it is first necessary to identify the nature of the order that has been obtained. Being an injunction restraining Claude from removing assets from the jurisdiction, it is a *Mareva* injunction. Note that you are asked to identify the 'best' advice. Answer [A] may have attractions for the dishonest, but would result in Claude being in contempt of Court, so is not advice that can be given to him. The Professional Standards Committee would not be impressed if this was your answer! There are elements of truth in answers [B] and [D]. Once a judge learns that the defendant has been notified of the claim, and particularly when the defendant has been notified that the plaintiff wants some form of security for its damages, the judge may well feel it is inappropriate for *Mareva* relief to be sought ex parte. Ex parte applications are always exceptional, and the matters mentioned in [B] and [D] may incline some judges into refusing ex parte *Mareva* relief. In such cases the plaintiff is forced into seeking the relief (if at all) inter partes. However, these are not reasons for *discharging Mareva* relief if the judge nevertheless decides to hear the application ex parte. The best answer is [C]. *Mareva* relief should only be granted where the defendant is the type of person who would dissipate his assets in order to frustrate any judgment the plaintiff may obtain (see *Civil Litigation Manual*, 13.4.4). Note the rather non-legal phrase used in answer [C] to describe this.

## CIVIL EVIDENCE

**18.** [A], [C] and [D] are all exceptions to the rule of finality of answers to collateral questions. As to [A], bias, see e.g. *Thomas* v *David* (1836) 7 C&P 350. As to [C], previous convictions, see s. 6 of the Criminal Procedure Act 1865, which applies to civil as well as criminal proceedings. As to [D], physical or mental disability affecting reliability, see *Toohey* v *Metropolitan Police Commissioner* [1965] AC 595. [B] is an 'invented' exception to the rule – there is no common-law or statutory authority to support it.

**19.** [A], [C] and [D] are all different ways of describing, accurately, the standard of proof required to discharge the legal burden of proof in a civil case. [B] is incorrect because if the probabilities are equal, the legal burden is not discharged – the scales have not been tipped. In *Miller* v *Minister of Pensions* [1947] 2 All ER 372, Denning J said: 'If the evidence is such that the tribunal can say: "we think it more probable than not", the burden is discharged, but if the probabilities are equal it is not.'

**20.** The general rule as to the incidence of the legal burden in civil cases is that he who asserts must prove. Is Marcus asserting that it *was* reasonably practicable to keep the premises safe, or are 5-X asserting that it was *not* reasonably practicable to keep the premises safe? The identical issue arose in *Nimmo* v *Alexander Cowan & Sons Ltd* [1968] AC 107, a Scottish civil case in which a majority of the House of Lords held that the defendant employers bore the burden of proving that it was not reasonably practicable to make and keep the premises safe, since on the face of the statute the incidence of the burden was unclear and the Court, in determining Parliament's intention, could go beyond the form of the enactment and look at policy considerations and the ease or difficulty that each of the parties would face in discharging the burden. Since 5-X bear the legal burden on the issue then, in accordance with the general rule, they also bear the evidential burden on that issue.

**21.** The common-law presumption of death can only be used to establish the fact of death; if a party wishes to establish that death occurred on a particular date or during a particular period, this calls for specific evidence additional to that required to establish the basic facts giving rise to this presumption. In *Re Phéne's Trusts* (1870) 5 Ch App 139 at p. 144, Giffard LJ said 'the law presumes a person who has not been heard of for 7 years to be dead, but in the absence of special circumstances it draws no presumption from the fact as to the particular period at which he died'. The authorities are in conflict as to the date on which the *fact* of death may be presumed, but that is a different matter.

**22.** This question concerns the admissibility of similar fact evidence in civil proceedings. The facts of the question are the same, in principle, as those of *Mood Music Publishing Co. Ltd v De Wolfe Publishing Ltd* [1976] Ch 119, an action concerning infringement of copyright in which the defendants alleged that the similarity between the work which they had produced and the work in which the plaintiffs owned the copyright was coincidental. The Court of Appeal held that evidence to show that on other occasions the defendants had produced works bearing a close resemblance to other works which were the subject of copyright was admissible to rebut the allegation of coincidence.

**23**.  [C] is incorrect because in civil cases evidence of the character of a party or a witness may be admissible not only when it is one of the very facts in issue, but also (i) if it is of sufficient relevance to the facts in issue (see, e.g., *Hales v Kerr* [1908] 2 KB 601 and other civil 'similar fact evidence' authorities) or (ii) sufficiently relevant to the credibility of a witness (see, e.g., the exceptions to the rule of finality of answers to collateral questions). [A] is well-established. As to the authority for [B], see per Lord Denning MR in *Helliwell v Piggott-Sims* [1980] FSR 582, CA. The authorities to support [D] are *Re Bramblevale Ltd* [1970] Ch 128, CA and *Dean v Dean* [1987] 1 FLR 517, CA.

**24**.   The Criminal Procedure Act 1865, s. 3, which applies to civil as well as criminal proceedings, provides that a party producing a witness who, in the opinion of the judge, proves hostile, may by leave of the judge prove that the witness has made at other times a statement inconsistent with his present testimony. That party may also ask the witness leading questions: *R v Thompson* [1976] 64 Cr App R 96. However, there is no authority to the effect that a party calling a witness who proves hostile may then cross-examine him on his previous convictions or may then adduce evidence to show that he is biased against that party.

**25**.   This question concerns the standard of proof appropriate to civil cases in which a party makes an allegation of fraud or criminal conduct. The facts of the question are identical, in principle, to those of *Hornal* v *Neuberger Products Ltd* [1957] 1 QB 247, CA, where it was held that on a charge of fraud, the appropriate standard is proof on a balance of probabilities, although the Court will naturally require a higher degree of probability than that which it would require when asking if, say, negligence is established. Denning LJ said: 'I think it would bring the law into contempt if a judge were to say on the issue of warranty he finds the statement was made, and that on the issue of fraud he finds it was not made.'

**26.** This question is designed to test your knowledge and comprehension of some of the basic terminology relating to the law of evidence. [C] is the correct answer because if the matter comes to trial, the facts contained in the allegation made by Mane-Line Hairdressers are the facts which they must prove in order to succeed in their defence. As to [A], 'collateral' is used to refer to (i) facts affecting the competence of a witness (e.g. the fact that a witness suffers from a mental handicap) (ii) facts affecting the credibility of a witness (e.g. the fact that a witness has a previous conviction for perjury) and (iii) preliminary facts. As to [B], the word 'preliminary' is used to refer to facts which have to be proved as a condition precedent to the admissibility of certain items of evidence. As to [D], judicial notice is generally taken of facts which are so notorious or of such common knowledge that they require no proof. The factual allegations made by Mane-Line Hairdressers can hardly be so described.

**27.** The authority to support [A] is the Children Act 1989, s. 96, whereby a child (a person under the age of 18) who is called a witness in any civil proceedings but does not understand the nature of an oath *may* be permitted to give unsworn evidence. [D] is well-established: the fact that a witness is compellable will not prevent him from refusing to answer specific questions if he is entitled so to refuse on the grounds of privilege. The authority to support [B] also illustrates why [C] is incorrect: the Evidence Amendment Act 1853, s. 1 (together with the Evidence Further Amendment Act 1869). Under these statutory provisions, which reversed the common-law rule to the contrary, a spouse of a party to civil proceedings is competent to testify for or against him.

**28**. [B] is the correct answer because the presumption of continuance of life is a presumption of fact. On the proof or admission of the primary or basic fact (that a person was alive on a certain date) it *may* be presumed, in the absence of sufficient evidence to the contrary, that that person was alive on a subsequent date – establishing the basic fact does *not* have the effect of placing either an evidential or a legal burden on the party against whom the presumption operates. The presumptions referred to in [A], [C] and [D] are all, by contrast, rebuttable presumptions of law, whereby on the proof or admission of the primary or basic fact(s), and in the absence of further evidence, another fact must be presumed, and the party against whom the presumption operates will then bear the legal burden of disproving the presumed fact or, as the case may be, an evidential burden to adduce some evidence in rebuttal of the presumed fact.

**29**. (i)  Under s. 3(1)(a) of the Civil Evidence Act 1968, where in any civil proceedings a previous inconsistent statement made by a witness has been put in evidence under s. 4 or s. 5 of the 1865 Act, it is admitted as evidence of any fact stated therein of which direct oral evidence by him would be admissible.

(ii)  Under s. 3(1)(b) of the 1968 Act, where in any civil proceedings a previous statement made by a witness is proved in order to rebut a suggestion that his evidence has been fabricated, that statement is admitted as evidence of any fact stated therein of which direct oral evidence by him would be admissible.

(iii)  Under s. 3(2) of the 1968 Act, where in any civil proceedings a witness is cross-examined on a document used by him to refresh his memory and the document is thereby made evidence in the proceedings, any statement made in that document by him shall be admissible as evidence of any fact stated therein of which direct oral evidence by him would be admissible.

**30**. [A] is correct because in civil cases, the Courts will generally admit evidence of similar facts if it is logically probative, i.e. if it is logically relevant in determining the matter which is in issue, provided that it is not oppressive or unfair to the other side: per Lord Denning MR in *Mood Music Publishing Co. Ltd* v *De Wolfe Publishing Ltd* [1976] Ch 119 at p. 127. Frank's previous behaviour is clearly relevant in deciding the issue of whether Frank was mistaken about the genuineness of the ring, and for this reason [C] is incorrect. As to [B], similar fact evidence which shows *only* that a defendant has a disposition to make fraudulent misrepresentations of the kind in question is inadmissible to prove that he made the fraudulent misrepresentation which is the subject of the action – see generally Lord Herschell's first proposition in *Makin* v *Attorney-General for New South Wales* [1894] AC 57, PC. As to [D], there is no authority to the effect that similar fact evidence, in order to be admissible, must relate to conduct which resulted in a conviction (or a conviction for a particular type of offence).

## CRIMINAL LITIGATION

**31.** Since the trial is a summary trial, the answer is contained in the Magistrates' Courts Rules 1981. Rule 13(1) allows the prosecutor to make an opening speech. Rule 13(2) provides that at the conclusion of the evidence for the prosecution, the accused may address the Court, whether or not he afterwards calls evidence (so [D] is wrong). Rule 13(4) provides that at the conclusion of the evidence for the defence, the accused may address the Court if he has not already done so. Thus, the prosecution have the right to make an opening speech, whereas the defence have the right to make either an opening speech or a closing speech. However, r. 13(5) provides that prosecution and defence may address the Court a second time, but only with the leave of the Court (so [A] is wrong and [B] is right).

Note that in a trial on indictment, counsel for the defence can only make an opening speech if the defence intend to call evidence as to the facts of the case other than or in addition to the evidence of the accused: *R* v *Hill* (1911) 7 Cr App R 1. [C] is wrong because the question states that the trial is a summary trial.

**32.** Detention without charge beyond 24 hours may be authorised by a superintendent if the offence is a serious arrestable offence; however, the superintendent can only authorise detention for a total of no more than 36 hours from the time of the suspect's arrival in the police station (so [B] is wrong). Detention beyond 36 hours may be ordered by a Magistrates' Court, but only to a maximum of 96 hours, so [A] is wrong (Police and Criminal Evidence Act 1984, s. 45(1)). After the expiry of the warrant of further detention issued by the magistrates, where the suspect has been in custody for the maximum period of 96 hours, the police must either charge him or release him on bail. The suspect cannot be re-arrested for the offence for which he was previously arrested unless new evidence justifying a further arrest has come to light since his release: Police and Criminal Evidence Act 1984, s. 43(19) (so [D] is wrong).

**33.**  Mike is a juvenile; Neville is an adult.

In [A] the adult is charged with aiding and abetting the juvenile to commit an offence (a summary offence, and so the adult has no choice but to be tried in the Magistrates' Court). In such a case, the adult Magistrates' Court may, in the exercise of its discretion, try the juvenile as well as the adult: Children and Young Persons Act 1993, s. 46(1)(b); if the adult Court does not try the juvenile it will remit him to the Youth Court for trial.

In [C] the adult and the juvenile are charged with separate, but closely connected, offences. Because the charge against one arises out of circumstances which are the same as or linked with the charge against the other, the adult Magistrates' Court has a discretion to try the juvenile as well as the adult: Children and Young Persons Act 1963, s. 18(b).

As to [D], where it becomes apparent during the course of the proceedings in an adult Magistrates' Court that the defendant who was believed to be an adult is in fact under 18, the Court may, if it thinks fit, complete the hearing: Children and Young Persons Act 1933, s. 46(1)(c). If the adult Court decides not to carry on with the hearing, the case will be remitted to the Youth Court.

That leaves [B]. The adult and the juvenile are jointly charged with the same offence. The offence is a summary one, and so the adult will have to be tried in the Magistrates' Court. Where an adult Magistrates' Court tries an adult and a juvenile is jointly charged with the adult, the adult Court must try the juvenile as well – there is no discretion to remit to the Youth Court: Children and Young Persons Act 1933, s. 46(1)(a).

**34.** Under s. 74 of the Supreme Court Act 1981, when the Crown Court is hearing an appeal it must consist of a High Court judge, a circuit judge, or a recorder, who must sit with not fewer than 2 nor more than 4 justices of the peace. Hence [C] is correct.

**35.** The charges cannot appear in the same information, as two separate offences are alleged, and so a single information would offend the rule against duplicity (Magistrates' Courts Rules 1981, r. 12(1)). If two or more defendants are charged on separate informations but the facts are connected, the informations may be heard together if the justices think fit. If consent to a joint trial is not forthcoming from all parties, the justices should consider the rival submissions and rule as they think right in the overall interests of justice. The justices should ask themselves whether it would be fair and just to the defendants to allow a joint trial. Only if the answer is clearly yes, should they order joint trial. Thus it is a matter for the discretion of the justices whether the defendants are tried separately or together (*Chief Constable of Norfolk* v *Clayton* [1983] 2 AC 473, at 491–2, per Lord Roskill) and [D] is correct.

**36.** Criminal damage where the value involved is less than £2,000 (to be increased to £5,000 when the Criminal Justice and Public Order Act comes into force) must be tried summarily: Magistrates' Courts Act 1980, s. 22. However, such criminal damage is one of the offences to which s. 40 of the Criminal Justice Act 1988 applies (see s. 40(3)). Under s. 140(1), if such an offence is founded on the same facts (or forms part of a series of offences of the same or similar character) as an indictable offence, a count alleging that summary offence may be included in the indictment along with the count alleging the indictable offence (so [A] is wrong).

In the present case, the criminal damage is founded on the same facts as the indictable offence of burglary (since they arise out of a single incident: *R v Barrell* (1979) 69 Cr App R 250). [D] is therefore correct.

Burglary is triable either way so Frank can elect Crown Court trial in respect of that offence and [C] is wrong. However, it is a matter for the prosecution whether the criminal damage appears on the indictment – the accused has no right to elect trial in respect of it (so [B] is wrong).

**37.** Section 6(5) of the Bail Act 1976 provides that an offence of absconding under s. 6 should be dealt with, 'either on summary conviction or as if it were a criminal contempt of Court'. In *Schiavo v Anderton* [1987] 1 WLR 79, it was held that a Bail Act offence is an offence which is triable only in the Court at which proceedings are to be heard in respect of which bail has been granted.

Frank has been committed to the Crown Court to stand trial. The substantive proceedings will thus be heard in the Crown Court. It follows that the Magistrates' Court has no jurisdiction over the Bail Act offence (so [D] is wrong). In *Schiavo* it was said that the Bail Act offence of absconding is not an indictable offence. It follows that there will not be a jury trial in respect of it (so [B] is wrong). Further, dealing with a Bail Act offence is not one of the situations prescribed in s. 74 of the Supreme Court Act 1981 where a Crown Court judge must sit with lay justices; thus, in dealing with a Bail Act offence, the judge sits alone (so [C] is wrong). [A] states the law correctly.

**38.** Normally, a person who pleads guilty in a Magistrates' Court may appeal to the Crown Court only against sentence (and not against conviction): Magistrates Courts Act 1980, s. 108. However, the plea of 'guilty but I have a defence' is an equivocal plea (compare *R v Durham Quarter Sessions ex parte Virgo* [1952] 2 QB 1, where a guilty plea was rendered equivocal by subsequent inconsistent mitigation). In such a case, the convicted person may appeal against conviction (so [B] is wrong). The proper procedure is for the Crown Court to decide whether the plea was indeed equivocal and, if it was (as is clearly the case in the present problem) it must remit the case for a trial to take place in the Magistrates' Court: *R* v *Plymouth Justices ex parte Hart* [1986] QB 950. Hence [A] and [C] are also wrong. [D] is correct.

**39**. There was nothing wrong with the decision of the Youth Court to try Idris as the Youth Court will often try cases which would be tried in the Crown Court if the offender were an adult.

Section 37(1) of the Magistrates' Courts Act 1980 provides that where a Magistrates' Court (in this context, this must mean a Youth Court) convicts an offender who has attained the age of 15 but is under 18 of an offence punishable with at least 6 months' imprisonment, the Court may, if it is of the opinion that the offender should be sentenced to a greater term of detention in a young offender institution than it has power to impose, commit him to the Crown Court for sentence. The fact that s. 37 says that the Youth Court may commit the offender to the Crown Court shows that [B], [C] and [D] are wrong.

**40**. Section 10 of the Criminal Appeal Act 1968 applies where an offender is sentenced in the Crown Court following committal for sentence under the Magistrates' Courts Act 1980, s. 38. Section 10(2) provides that appeal lies to the Court of Appeal if the Crown Court passes a custodial sentence of 6 months or more, or (inter alia) disqualifies the offender from holding or obtaining a driving licence. As the Crown Court has imposed a custodial sentence of less than 6 months, there is no appeal to the Court of Appeal against that sentence.

**41**. A juvenile ought to be tried summarily unless:

(i)    the charge is one of homicide;

(ii)    he or she is charged jointly with an adult who is to be tried on indictment, and it is in the interests of justice to commit both for trial;

(iii) the offence is one of those covered by s. 53(2) of the Children and Young Persons Act 1933 (maximum sentence 14 years or more for an adult, or one of certain specified offences, e.g. indecent assault on a woman) and the Court considers a sentence under that section might be appropriate. (See the Magistrates' Court Act 1980, s. 24(1).)

Here the only exception to the general rule which might apply is (iii). The stated maximum sentence is such that the offence of burglary of a dwelling falls within the Children and Young Persons Act 1933, s. 53(2).

It follows that [A] is right. [B] is wrong, as the magistrates have a discretion and must themselves decide whether the offences are too serious. [C] is wrong, since a sentence under s. 53(2) would be lawful. [D] is wrong, since juveniles can be tried in the Crown Court for burglary of a dwelling.

**42.** Summary trials can and often do take place in the absence of the defendant. The Magistrates' Court Act 1980, s. 11 deals with the situation where the defendant fails to appear, It gives the magistrates a discretion to proceed in his or her absence. If they do proceed, a not guilty plea must be entered.

Hence [A] is wrong since the magistrates are not obliged to adjourn. [B] is right. They do have a discretion to hear the case on the basis of a not guilty plea. [C] is wrong in its use of the word 'must': they have a discretion on the question of whether to proceed. [D] is wrong, since, if they do proceed, they have no discretion as to the plea – they must deal with it on the basis of a not guilty plea.

**43.** Under s. 36 of the Police and Criminal Evidence Act 1984, the decision to detain must be taken by the custody officer, who should hold at least the rank of sergeant. There must then be periodic reviews of detention – those of relevance here are 6 hours after the original decision and 9 hours after that. The review officer must hold the rank of inspector or above.

[A] is therefore wrong: there was no need to hold reviews at the times stated in that option. [B] is wrong for the same reason. [C] is right, The officer deciding to detain should have been at least a sergeant; the officer reviewing should have been at least an inspector. [D] is wrong, since Jacob does have a legitimate ground of complaint.

**44.** The procedure for judicial review is contained in s. 31 of the Supreme Court Act 1981, and in the Rules of the Supreme the Court 1965, Ord. 53. Kevin's first step must be to make an application for leave to apply for judicial review. This is done to a single High Court judge, with grounds supported by an affidavit. It is usually decided on the papers, and is in any event ex parte. Notice to the other side need only be given later, if leave is granted.

Hence [A], [C] and [D] are wrong, since the question specifically asks what Kevin should do *first*, and there is no need to notify the prosecution or the Magistrates' Court at this initial stage. [B] is correct. In the first instance, the application goes to the High Court only.

**45.** Where a defendant is convicted by the magistrates and appeals to the Crown Court, sentence falls to be reconsidered, even if the appeal is against conviction only. When reconsidering sentence, the Crown Court can reduce it, leave it unaltered, or increase it to the maximum which the magistrates could have imposed (Supreme Court Act 1981, s. 81). The Crown Court can also make such order as to costs as it thinks just.

So [A] is wrong, since the Crown Court has the power to increase sentence. [B] is wrong, since it can both increase sentence and order him to pay costs. [C] is correct. [D] is wrong. The power of the Crown Court to increase sentence is limited to the maximum the magistrates could have imposed (6 months for a single count of ABH) and not the maximum applicable to trial on indictment (5 years).

**46.** [A] complies with s. 8 of the Criminal Justice Act 1967, which, re-establishing the presumption of intention as a presumption of *fact,* provides that the jury, in deciding whether a person has committed an offence – (a) shall not be bound in law to infer that he intended or foresaw a result of his actions by reason only of its being a natural and probable consequence of those actions; but (b) shall decide whether he did intend or foresee that result by reference to all the evidence, drawing such inferences from the evidence as appear proper in the circumstances. None of [B] [C] or [D] complies with s. 8. [D] also erroneously suggests that Gareth has the legal burden of disproving the requisite intent.

**47.** [B] is correct (and [C] is incorrect) because under s. 10 of the Criminal Justice Act 1967, a formal admission may be made at the proceedings by or on behalf of the prosecutor or defendant, and *R* v *Lewis* [1989] Crim LR 61, CA, establishes that in Court, counsel may formally admit a fact under s. 10 *orally.* [A] is incorrect because under s. 10(2)(b) it is if the admission is made *otherwise than in Court* that it shall be in writing. [D] is doubly incorrect: the formal admission *is* admissible; and even assuming (wrongly) that it is inadmissible, at common law a judge has no discretionary power to admit evidence which is inadmissible in law.

**48.** Ghisha, the wife of the accused Fred, is competent to give evidence for the prosecution: Police and Criminal Evidence Act 1984, s. 80(1)(a). She is not compellable because the case falls outside s. 80(3) of the 1984 Act, which sets out the only circumstances in which the spouse of an accused shall be compellable to give evidence for the prosecution. Irene is competent and compellable pursuant to the general rule at common law that all witnesses are competent and compellable. Her position is not governed by s. 80 of the 1984 Act because she is not 'the wife . . . of the accused' – her husband, Harry, by pleading guilty, has ceased to be an accused.

**49.** [A] is incorrect because although in a summing-up a judge should not attempt any gloss upon the meaning of 'reasonable doubt', because it is more likely to confuse than help the jury, in exceptional cases, as when the jury return to Court and ask for a further direction, the jury should be given help: see *R v Yap Chuan Ching* (1976) 63 Cr App R 7, CA. The direction in [B] has been expressly disapproved: *R v Stafford* and *R v Luvaglio* (1968) 53 Cr App R 1. The direction in [C] suggests too low a standard of proof: *R v Gray* (1973) 58 Cr App R 177. The direction in [D] was upheld by the Privy Council in *Walters v R* [1969] 2 AC 26.

**50.** [A] is incorrect because even if the evidence of discovery of the magazines could be said to show Michael's disposition to commit the kind of offence with which he is charged – which it does not – it would be inadmissible under Lord Herschell's first proposition in *Makin v Attorney-General for New South Wales* [1894] AC 57, PC. See also per Neill LJ in *R v Lunt* (1987) 85 Cr App R 241, CA, at p. 245. [B] is incorrect: if Michael's defence was that he had touched Nora accidentally, there might be a case for a submission that the evidence goes to rebut it, but the evidence clearly does not rebut a mere denial – see *R v Lewis* (1983) 76 Cr App R 33. [D] is incorrect because however relevant this evidence may be – and views may differ – it is certainly not 'highly' relevant. As to [C], the correct answer, the evidence in this case does not have sufficiently probative value to outweigh its obvious prejudicial effect.

**51.** Under s. 2(2) of the Homicide Act 1957, an express statutory exception to the general rule laid down in *Woolmington v DPP* [1935] AC 462, HL, the accused bears the legal burden of establishing the defence of diminished responsibility on a charge of murder. The defence will also bear the evidential burden, in accordance with the general rule that a party bearing the legal burden on an issue will also bear the evidential burden on that issue. Where the legal burden on an issue is borne by the accused, it is discharged by proof on a balance of probabilities: see *R v Carr-Briant* [1943] KB 607, CCA and *R v Dunbar* [1958] 1 QB 1.

**52.** The authority to support [A] is the Sexual Offences (Amendment) Act 1976, s. 2(1). The authority to support [B] is s. 2(2) of that Act. The authority to support [D] is the dictum of May J in *R* v *Lawrence* [1977] Crim LR 492 at pp. 492–3, approved by the Court of Appeal in *R* v *Mills* (1978) 68 Cr App R 327. There is no authority to support [C].

**53.**   As to [A], the authorities have consistently stated that it is a matter of discretion for the judge whether to make any comment at all on the failure of the accused to testify: see e.g. *R* v *Rhodes* [1899] 1 QB 77 at p. 88 and *R* v *Harris* (1986) 84 Cr App R 75, CA. [B] is possible under s. 10 of the Criminal Justice Act 1967. [C] is possible under s. 73 of the Police and Criminal Evidence Act 1984. As to [D], the situation is not governed by s. 1(f) of the Criminal Evidence Act 1898. Section 1(f) begins: 'A person charged and called as a witness . . .', but Tom does not give evidence. Thus if the accused does not testify and the defence cross-examine a prosecution witness as to his bad character, but do not adduce evidence as to the accused's good character and do not cross-examine prosecution witnesses with a view to establishing the accused's good character, evidence of the accused's bad character may not be called for the prosecution; the accused has not put his own character in issue, but that of the prosecution witness – see *R* v *Butterwasser* [1948] 1 KB 4, CCA.

**54.**   The statement in (i) is correct because the general rule is that a witness may not be asked in examination-in-chief about former statements made by him and consistent with his evidence in the proceedings: see *R* v *Roberts* [1942] 1 All ER 187. The statement in (ii) is correct because one of the exceptions to the general rule arises if, in cross-examination, it is suggested to the witness that his version of events is a recent invention or fabrication, in which case evidence of a prior statement to the same effect will be admissible, in re-examination, to support his credit: see, e.g., *R* v *Oyesiku* (1971) 56 Cr App R 240, CA.

**55.**   [A] is incorrect because previous identification of the accused is a well-established exception to the general rule against previous consistent or self-serving statements. [B] is incorrect (and [D] correct) because it is generally undesirable and improper first to invite a witness to identify the accused from the witness-box, i.e. to make a 'dock identification' (see *R v Cartwright* (1914) 10 Cr App R 219); if there has been a previous out-of-Court identification of the accused by the witness, the best and usual practice is to elicit evidence of the previous identification *before* then asking the witness whether that person is in the Court-room. [C] is incorrect because if the witness cannot give evidence identifying the accused in Court, there is no testimony with which the previous identification can be consistent.

**56**. [B] is incorrect because the evidence is clearly relevant to the issue whether Alf's conduct was deliberate or accidental. There is no authority to support [D]. [C] is the correct answer (and [A] incorrect) because the evidence may be admitted on the same reasoning employed in (i) 'similar fact' cases such as *Makin* v *Attorney-General for New South Wales* [1894] AC 57, PC, and *R v Smith* (1915) 11 Cr App R 229, CCA (given the defence, the magnitude of the coincidence involved) or *DPP* v *Boardman* [1975] AC 421, HL (evidence so very relevant that to exclude it would be an affront to common sense) or (ii) *R v P* [1991] 3 All ER 337, HL (the evidence of the victims is so related that the evidence of the first provides strong enough support for the evidence of the second to make it just to admit it notwithstanding its prejudicial effect).

**57**. Jane is competent to give evidence for the prosecution: Police and Criminal Evidence Act 1984, s. 80(1)(a). She is not compellable because the case falls outside s. 80(3) of the 1984 Act, which sets out the only circumstances in which the spouse of an accused shall be compellable to give evidence for the prosecution. For these reasons, [C] is correct (and [B] incorrect). As to [A] and [D], in *R v Pitt* [1982] 3 All ER 63, CA, it was held that if a wife is a competent but not compellable witness for the prosecution, her choice whether or not to give evidence for the prosecution is not lost because she has already made a witness statement or given evidence at the committal proceedings.

**58**. Michelle is competent for the prosecution under s. 80(1)(a) of the Police and Criminal Evidence Act 1984, and compellable for the prosecution under both parts of s. 80(3)(a) of the 1984 Act ('the offence charged involves an assault on . . . the wife . . . of the accused or a person who was at the material time under the age of 16'). For these reasons, [B] is correct (and [A], [C] and [D] incorrect). As to [A], the fact that Michelle is separated from John makes no difference: they are still married. Even if they were no longer married, the answer would be the same, because a person who is no longer married to the accused shall be competent and compellable to give evidence as if that person and the accused had never been married: s. 80(5) of the 1984 Act.

**59.** As to [A], there is no authority to suggest that an accused may be cross-examined on previous convictions if 'not a credible witness'. As to [B], Morgan could be cross-examined on his previous convictions if he had cast imputations on the character of a prosecution witness (under s. 1(f)(ii) of the Criminal Evidence Act 1898), but on the facts given no such imputation has been cast. [C] is correct because the words 'to show' in s. 1(f) of the 1898 Act mean 'to make known', 'to reveal' or 'to disclose', and therefore cross-examination will not be prohibited because the jury are already aware of the fact that he has been in trouble with the police before: *Jones v DPP* [1962] AC 635. [D] is incorrect because even if the previous conviction could be said to show Morgan's general propensity towards offences of a sexual nature, it would be inadmissible under Lord Herschell's first proposition in *Makin v Attorney-General for New South Wales* [1894] AC 57, PC.

**60.** [A] is incorrect: see Lord Herschell's first proposition in *Makin v Attorney-General for New South Wales* [1894] AC 57, PC – see the answer to Question 59 above. [B] is correct (and [C] incorrect) for two reasons. First, because the allegation of the extra-marital relationship with Melanie, a prosecution witness, constitutes an imputation on her character for the purposes of s. 1(f)(ii) of the Criminal Evidence Act 1898: *cf R v Bishop* [1975] QB 274, CA. Secondly, Owen has lost his shield under s. 1(f)(ii) by denying Melanie's evidence that he is a complete stranger to her – his evidence that they were having an affair necessarily implies that she has given false evidence against him: *cf R v Britzman; R v Hall* [1983] 1 WLR

350, CA. As to [D], as a matter of law, i.e. ignoring any question of discretionary exclusion, s. 1(f)(ii) permits cross-examination even when the casting of an imputation on the character of a prosecution witness is necessary to enable the accused to establish his defence: *Selvey* v *DPP* [1970] AC 304, HL and *R* v *Bishop*, ibid.

# APPENDIX 4

# NOTE-FORM ANSWERS
# TO MCT – PART 2

### CIVIL LITIGATION

**1.** In questions like this one it is often useful to compile a short chronology:

| | |
|---|---|
| September 1988 | Accrual of cause of action |
| July 1994 | Service of writ |
| September 1994 | Expiry of limitation period |
| October 1994 | Service of Defence |
| November 1994 | Close of Pleadings |
| March 1995 | Today |

It will be noticed that the entries for September 1994 and November 1994 are calculated from dates which are given. Richard's proposed amendment is to change the company being sued, and is being sought after the expiry of the limitation period. Generally new parties cannot be substituted after the expiry of the limitation period: Limitation Act 1980, s. 35(3). However, substitution may be allowed after the expiry of the limitation period if it is necessary for the determination of the original action (Limitation Act 1980, s. 35(5)(b)), and substitution may be regarded as necessary if the original party's name was given in mistake for the new party's name (Limitation Act 1980, s. 35(6) (a)). Under RSC Ord. 20, r. 5(3) the mistake must be genuine and not such as to cause reasonable doubt as to the identity of the person intended to be sued. Hence the answer is [A]. Answer [C] reflects the general rule in the Limitation Act 1980, s. 35(3), but ignores s. 35(5) and (6). The other answers were all dreamed up for the MCT. Despite the complexity of the above answer, this is a reasonably straightforward question.

**2.** This question requires knowledge of the bases of taxation of costs. Answer [A] describes the indemnity basis. Answer [B] has been dreamt up, but has its attractions because of the general discretionary nature of costs *orders*. Answer [C] describes the statutory protection on costs of a legally assisted party by virtue of the Legal Aid Act 1988, s. 17. The correct answer is [D], see *Civil Litigation Manual*, 31.5.2.2.

**3.** It is first necessary to identify the type of enforcement procedure being described in the answers, and then to consider the mechanics of how they are operated. Answer [A] is the writ fieri facias; [B] is the writ of delivery; and [D] is the writ of possession. All of these are enforced by the sheriff. Answer [C] describes the garnishee order, which, when made absolute, requires a non-party (the garnishee) who owes money to the judgment debtor to pay that money to the judgment creditor. This does not require the intervention of the sheriff. Consequently [C] is the correct answer.

**4.** Chronology:

| | |
|---|---|
| 3 June 1989 | Accrual of cause of action |
| 30 November 1994 | Writ issued |
| 6 March 1995 | Writ sent by post (not served) |
| 29 March 1995 | Today: (a) Writ returned marked 'Gone away' |
| | (b) Validity of writ expires |
| 3 June 1995 | Expiry of limitation period. |

The question asks what 'immediate' action should be taken. Answer [A] is not very practical: it would work only if there was some information as to the defendant's whereabouts so that personal service could be effected. As to answer [B], it may be sensible to issue a new writ and write-off the present one. However, there is no need to do this 'immediately' as the limitation period does not expire until June, and as the writ will be valid only for 4 months, given that the defendant has disappeared, there would appear to be practical reasons for delaying issuing again for the time being. In any event, the client may not relish the idea of another £100 issue fee etc. The other option is to renew the existing writ. Today is the last day of its validity, so if the application is delayed until tomorrow it will be necessary not only to show a good reason for renewing (problems in effecting service should amount to this), but also to give a satisfactory explanation for the delay. It therefore makes sense to apply immediately. The difference between [C] and [D] lies in the procedure to be adopted. The difficulty in this question lies principally in the fact that it is a multiple-stage question. By definition there is no defendant on the record at this stage, so the application to renew has to be made ex parte as opposed to on notice (inter partes). Answer [C] describes the ex parte procedure and is correct; answer [D] describes what would be the inter partes procedure.

**5.** This is a question on summoning witnesses, for which see *Civil Litigation Manual*, 29.3.5. Subpoenas are used in the High Court, whereas witness orders are used in the County Courts. A *subpoena duces tecum* requires the witness to produce documents, so the answer is [B]; a witness required to give oral testimony may be served with a *subpoena ad testificandum*.

**6.** Proceedings may be commenced in England against Daisy Bell only if the rules on seeking leave under RSC Ord. 11 are satisfied. The USA is not a party to the Brussels or Lugano Conventions, so answer [C] is wrong. The fact the *plaintiffs* are incorporated here does not give the English Courts jurisdiction (answer [A]). The facts that the contract is governed by English law and that the English Courts have been given jurisdiction provide grounds for granting leave to issue proceedings and to serve outside the jurisdiction (RSC Ord. 11, r. 1(1)(d)(iii) and (iv)) see *Civil Litigation Manual*, 9.2.4.1). Although this is not all that is required (see 9.2.4), there are grounds for seeking leave, answer [B].

**7.** Chronology:

| | |
|---|---|
| 7 December 1992 | Cause of action accrued |
| 6 April 1994 | Laura served Request for Further and Better Particulars of the Statement of Claim |
| 20 December 1994 | Order to provide the requested particulars within 21 days |
| 10 January 1995 | Expiry of the 21 days |
| 29 March 1995 | Today. |

Laura wants to dismiss Winston's action for want of prosecution (not striking out for abuse of process [C] or discontinuance [D]) on the ground he has failed to provide the requested particulars. *Birkett* v *James* [1978] AC 297 makes clear that dismissal applications fall into 2 categories:

(a) For inordinate and inexcusable delay. There are a number of conditions, one being that generally the limitation period must have expired. The exceptions to this rule are extremely limited (see *Civil Litigation Manual*, 21.3.3.3). The limitation period is 6 years as this is a breach of contract action, so will expire in 1998. Hence answer [B] is not the practical answer.

(b) For breach of a peremptory (otherwise known as an 'unless') order. There has been no such order so far in this action, so the next thing Laura should do is to apply for one, answer [A] (see 21.3.2).

**8.** The rules on disclosure of witnesses statements have developed over recent years. The original position was that written statements taken by solicitors from potential witnesses in advance of trial were protected from disclosure to the other side or the Court by legal professional privilege, answer [D]. Then, some of the specialist Courts within the High Court experimented with mutual exchange of witnesses' statements, answer [A]. More recently, rules were made covering all High Court and County Court actions under which the parties could apply for an order (usually on the summons for directions or pre-trial review) for the exchange of witnesses' statements, answer [C]. Early decisions under these rules were to the effect that mutual disclosure was to be the normal order, and it soon became clear that mutual disclosure should be included among the automatic directions which apply in most County Court actions and High Court personal injuries actions. This change was brought in when the rules were recast in 1992, so, as things now stand, the correct answer is [B].

**9**. An appeal from a final decision by a County Court judge is Court of Appeal, answer [D]. See *Civil Litigation Manual*, Table 35.1. For some inexplicable reason students have always had difficulties with this question. Of those getting it wrong, almost equal numbers chose each of the other answers.

**10**. Mr Brown's report was obtained and paid for by the plaintiff, and has been disclosed to the defendant. After a change of solicitors a 'better' report has been obtained for the plaintiff from another expert. Having been disclosed, the defendant is entitled to put the first report in evidence: RSC Ord. 38, r. 42 (*Civil Litigation Manual*, 26.12.2), so answer [D] is correct. Before disclosure it was protected by legal professional privilege, answer [C]. Answers [A] and [B] are based on concepts from other areas.

**11**. Insisting that the applicant merely had to show a serious issue to be tried on the merits was the main point of the *American Cyanamid* decision (see *Civil Litigation Manual*, 12.3.1.1). Consequently the correct answer is [B]. Before *American Cyanamid* the accepted principle was that a party seeking an interlocutory injunction had to establish a prima facie case on the merits of its claim, answer [A]. This often meant the parties felt constrained to attempt to prove the merits of the claim and defence in voluminous affidavits and exhibits, resulting in very long and expensive interlocutory hearings. Avoiding such a waste of resources before trial was the main motivation behind the *American Cyanamid* decision. Answers [C] and [D] are also concerned with the standard of proof, but put the test too high.

**12**. By virtue of RSC Ord. 114, r. 4, once an order for a reference to the European Court of Justice has been made the English proceedings are stayed until the European Court has given its preliminary ruling on the question referred to it. Rulings given by the European Court are in a general form, so, although the English Court is bound by the ruling, it is left to the English Court to decide the English proceedings in the light of the ruling of the European Court. Hence the answer is [A]; answers [B] to [D] were dreamt up for the purposes of the MCT.

**13**. This should be a straightforward question on a very practical aspect of the law on costs. Unfortunately it has had one of the highest 'failure rates' of all the Civil Litigation questions used over the years. The answer is [B] see *Civil Litigation Manual*, 31.3.2.4, paragraph (b). Many students were apparently getting confused with legal aid certificates.

**14**. It seems certain that the document will be hearsay. A Civil Evidence Act 1968 notice should therefore be served within 21 days after setting down for trial. Being unfit to attend by reason of one's bodily condition is one of the reasons specified in RSC Ord. 38, r. 25, and will prevent the other side serving an effective counternotice. Hence the answer is [A]. Answer [B] is based on criminal procedure. Answer [C] is unnecessary: death is not the only reason in RSC Ord. 38, r. 25. Answer [D] is nonsense.

**15**. The basic rule is that a plaintiff has a completely free choice as to whether to commence proceedings in either the High Court or a County Court, see *Civil Litigation Manual*, 1.1.3.4. There are a number of detailed rules covering specific types of proceedings, but none of them applies to an ordinary action for breach of contract like the action in this question. Hence the correct answer is [C]. The figure of £25,000 in answers [B] and [D] is the threshold used for determining whether actions should be transferred from the High Court for trial in the County Courts, but that is not directly relevant to the question of commencement.

**16.** Where, as here, the plaintiff sues on 2 causes of action, the defendant has the choice when paying in of making:

(a)   a single global payment in respect of both causes of action; or

(b)   individual payments in respect of each cause of action.

(See *Civil Litigation Manual*, 22.2.3.) The defendant has a free choice in the matter, but the Notice of Payment In must make it clear what the defendant has done. Hence answers [A] and [D] are wrong. When the defendant makes a global payment in (as here), the plaintiff is stuck with it unless he can establish that the payment in in that form causes embarrassment (see 22.2.4). Accordingly, the correct answer is [B].

**17.**   This is the longest question on the Civil Litigation parts of the MCTs in this book, and is representative of the longer questions that appear on the MCTS. Do not be surprised to find more than one question of this length on any single paper: they will usually be balanced by shorter questions. A careful analysis of the facts is especially important in questions of this type, and setting out a short chronology is an essential first step.

Chronology:

| | |
|---|---|
| 27 February 1989 | Cause of action accrued |
| 7 November 1994 | Writ issued |
| December 1994 | Defendant's solicitors informed writ issued |
| 4 January 1995 | Defendant's solicitors, letter |
| 27 February 1995 | Limitation expired |
| 6 March 1995 | Writ expired |
| 29 March 1995 | Today |

Surprisingly, simply serving and hoping as referred to in answer [A] *is* an option. Serving the writ after the expiry of the limitation period and the expiry of its period of validity does not make service a nullity, but merely an irregularity (RSC Ord. 2, r. 1). A defendant who does not take the point will be regarded as having waived the irregularity. In any event, the plaintiff can apply for the irregularity to be cured (see *Civil Litigation Manual*, 1.2.5), even if it will be quite a difficult task to persuade the Court to cure these particular irregularities. Therefore we need to look at the other answers.

It is established that continuing negotiations with nothing more does not constitute a good reason for extending the validity of a writ: *The Mouna* [1991] 2 Lloyds Rep 221, CA (see 20.5.3). If, being marked 'without prejudice', the letter of 4 January 1995 could not be looked at, answer [B] would be correct. However, such communications are in fact looked at in interlocutory proceedings precisely because they can explain apparent inactivity: *Family Housing Association (Manchester) Ltd* v *Michael Hyde and Partners* [1993] 1 WLR 354, CA. Answer [C] is wrong because it just considers the need to show a good reason for renewing (here the request to postpone service in the 'without prejudice' letter). On the other hand [D] is correct, because it also considers the need to explain the delay after 6 March, the expiry of the 4-month period of validity of the writ, before applying for the extension.

**18**.    This question concerns the date of knowledge provisions of the Limitation Act 1980, s. 14. In April 1990 William did not know he had been injured. At his medical examination he found out he had a lung injury (which would manifest itself at a later date) which would have justified the institution of proceedings. He already knows it was due to the chemical escape the previous year, and he always knew the identity of the tortfeasor (his employer). Time therefore began to run in January 1991, answer [B] (or possibly slightly before January 1991, see *Broadley* v *Guy Clapham & Co.* [1994] 4 All ER 439). Knowledge that he had a good legal cause of action, which he obtained after consulting the solicitor (answer [D]), is irrelevant, as expressly provided by s. 14.

**19**.    Like most summary judgment questions, it is easy to go wrong on this question. By virtue of the Sale of Goods Act 1979, s. 53, a defendant being sued for the price of goods sold is entitled to set-off a counterclaim for damages in respect of the breach of the conditions implied by the Act, including the implied term as to merchantable quality. We are told the facts are not in dispute, so the District Judge will almost certainly act on the facts deposed to in the affidavits. We are told the counterclaim is worth £2,500. Therefore there is no defence to the balance between the price of £4,000 and the value of the counterclaim, £2,500, which means judgment should be entered for Sally in the sum of £1,500. As Brian has a set-off defence to the balance, he should be granted unconditional leave to defend for that part of the claim. Thus the correct answer is [C].

**20**. This question needs careful thought. The Master has indicated that the defendants' case is marginally stronger than the plaintiffs'. Prospects of success should only be taken into account where one side's case is clearly stronger than that of the other. Otherwise applications for security for costs will degenerate into detailed enquiries into the merits, see *Porzelack KG* v *Porzelack (UK) Ltd* [1987] 1 All ER 1074. Consequently, answers [A] and [C] are wrong. Answer [B] is wrong because the plaintiffs' insolvency is not the only factor to be taken into account. Answer [D] is the best answer because it gets the principle correct on the question of the merits of the respective claims, and also takes into account other relevant factors (defendants' conduct contributing to plaintiffs' insolvency and stifling a genuine claim (the merits of the plaintiffs' claim have to be considered, despite what has been said above, for this more limited purpose)). Notice that the way the Master decides this case (whether to grant or refuse security for costs) does not affect the correctness or otherwise of answers [C] and [D] given the way in which they are phrased. This is inevitable in an area, like this one, where the Court has a very wide discretion.

**21**. Careful analysis is required for this question. You act for the plaintiff. You have been successful, and want to get your costs from the legally aided defendant. You cannot get your costs from the Legal Aid Board under the Legal Aid Act 1988, s. 18, answer [D], because the proceedings, which were at first instance, were *not* instituted by the legally assisted person (Legal Aid Act 1988, s. 18(4)(b)). [C] is wrong because Martin is protected from the usual costs order by the Legal Aid Act 1988, s. 17. [B] is wrong because the protection is not absolute. The usual order made in these circumstances is that stated in answer [A], which gives the assisted person protection, but allows the successful party to seek leave to enforce the costs order if the assisted person comes into money at some stage in the future.

**22.** Once a year has elapsed without any step being taken in a High Court action, the plaintiff can only resume the litigation after giving the defendant 1 month's Notice of Intention to Proceed. *Civil Litigation Manual*, 21.4. Answer [B] has simply been dreamt up. Answer [C] is nonsense – time runs for limitation purposes from accrual of the cause of action to the issue of process: *Thompson v Brown* [1981] 1 WLR 747, HL. Having been given Notice of Intention to Proceed Deborah is not powerless (answer [A]), but can apply to dismiss for want of prosecution (answer [D]), there being considerable delay and the limitation period having expired. She will also have to show prejudice or the impossibility of having a fair trial (see 21.3.3.1), which is not always easy.

**23.** A relatively straightforward question to finish off. Clearly this is an *Anton Piller* order enabling the plaintiff by its supervising solicitor to search for and take delivery of relevant documents. Consequently answer [A] was the one to select.

## CIVIL EVIDENCE

**24.** This question concerns proof of an oral hearsay statement admissible under s. 2 of the Civil Evidence Act 1968. Section 2(3) provides that 'Where in any civil proceedings a statement which was made otherwise than in a document is admissible by virtue of this section, no evidence other than direct oral evidence by the person who made the statement or any person who heard or otherwise perceived it being made shall be admissible for the purpose of proving it'. Thus the statement can only be proved by the evidence of Quentin or Robert – Sylvia and Timothy did not make the statement and neither heard nor otherwise perceived it being made. However, if Quentin, the maker of the statement, is called as a witness, the statement shall not be given in evidence without the leave of the Court – see the Civil Evidence Act 1968, s. 2(2).

**25.** Under s. 31(1) of the Theft Act 1968, questions must be answered in proceedings for the recovery or administration of any property, for the execution of any trust or for an account of any property or dealings with property, notwithstanding that compliance may expose the witness (or his spouse) to a charge for an offence under the Theft Act, but the answers may not be used in proceedings for any such offence.

**26.** [B] is correct (and [A] and [C] incorrect) because David's evidence constitutes statements of opinion by him on relevant matters (speed, distance, and the suddenness of braking) on which he is not qualified to give expert evidence, all of which have been made as a way of conveying relevant facts. The evidence is therefore admissible under s. 3(2) of the Civil Evidence Act 1972. [D] is incorrect because in civil proceedings admissible non-expert opinion evidence may relate to the ultimate issues in the case – 'relevant matter', for the purposes of s. 3(2), includes an issue in the proceedings in question: s. 3(3) of the 1972 Act.

**27.** [B] is correct (and [A] incorrect) because of RSC Ord. 38, r. 29(2), whereby the Court may exercise its discretion to admit a statement falling within s. 2(1) of the 1968 Act notwithstanding that the party seeking to admit it has failed to comply with any requirement of a counter-notice, if a refusal to do so might oblige that party to call as a witness at the trial an opposing party or a person who is or was at the material time the servant or agent of an opposing party. There is no authority to support [C]. As to [D], even if the statement contains damaging admissions, it can only be tendered against Damien as an informal admission if the communication in which it was made was authorised, whether expressly or by implication, by Damien, but on the facts Edward had no actual or imputed authority to speak on Damien's behalf: see *Wagstaff* v *Wilson* (1832) 4 B & Ad 339.

**28.** The letter is inadmissible for the reasons contained in [C] (not [B] or [D]) because provided that there is some dispute, and an attempt is being made to settle it, the Courts are prepared to infer that the attempt was 'without prejudice', even if that expression was not actually used: see *Chocoladenfabriken Lindt & Sprungli AG* v *The Nestlé Co. Ltd* [1978] RPC 287, a case which also explains why [A] is incorrect.

**29**. [B] is the best description, because of the Civil Evidence Act 1968, s. 11, which (a) reverses the rule in *Hollington* v *Hewthorn & Co. Ltd* [1943] KB 587 CA, and (b) operates as a persuasive presumption. Thus under s. 11(1), the fact that a person has been convicted of an offence by a UK Court shall be admissible to prove, where to do so is relevant to any issue in the proceedings, that he committed that offence; and under s. 11(2), if in any civil proceedings a person by virtue of the section is proved to have been convicted of the offence, he shall be taken to have committed it unless the contrary is proved. See also RSC Ord. 18, r. 7A(1) and (3).

**30**. Legal professional privilege enables a client to claim privilege for, inter alia, statements or reports received from potential witnesses (including experts) provided that the dominant purpose of the preparation of the statements or reports was submission to a legal adviser for use in relation to anticipated or pending litigation. If there was another equally important (or dominant) purpose, for example to inform the client about the cause of an accident so as to prevent such an accident in the future, the statement or report cannot be withheld: see generally *Waugh* v *British Railways Board* [1980] AC 521, HL. There is no authority to support [B], [C] or [D].

**31**. [C] is incorrect because the original supplier of the information is subject to the condition that he 'had or may reasonably be supposed to have had, personal knowledge of the matters dealt with in that information' and in appropriate circumstances, the Court will infer that this condition is satisfied: see *Knight* v *David* [1971] 1 WLR 1671. The opening words of s. 4(1) of the Civil Evidence Act 1968 are the authority for [A]. The authority to support [B] is s. 1(1) of the Civil Evidence Act 1972. [D] is supported by the closing words of s. 4(1) of the 1968 Act, which state that the information may be supplied to the compiler of the record 'indirectly through one or more intermediaries each acting under a duty'.

**32**. [A] is incorrect because provided that an expert states the assumed facts upon which his opinion is based, he need have no personal knowledge of the facts upon which he does base his opinion: see *Beckwith* v *Sydebotham* (1807) 1 Camp 116. Equally, the expert, as a part of the process of forming his opinion, may refer not only to his own research, tests or articles, but also to such research and articles etc. by others which form part of the general body of knowledge within the relevant field of expertise: see *Davie* v *Edinburgh Magistrates* 1953 SC 34. [B] is incorrect because in civil proceedings the rule against experts expressing an opinion on the ultimate issues has been abolished by statute: see the Civil Evidence Act 1972, s. 3(1) and (3). [C] is also incorrect: see *H* v *Schering Chemicals Ltd* [1983] 1 WLR 143. For all the above reasons, [D] is correct.

**33.** The reason why [A] is correct is to be found in *Science Research Council* v *Nassé* [1980] AC 1028, HL, where is was held that there is no principle by which documents are protected from discovery by reason of confidentiality alone but, in the exercise of its discretion to order discovery, a tribunal may take into account the fact that disclosure will involve a breach of confidentiality. The ultimate test is whether discovery is necessary for disposing fairly of the proceedings. If so, discovery must be ordered notwithstanding confidentiality, and in order to decide whether discovery is necessary notwithstanding confidentiality, a tribunal should inspect the documents. A claim to public interest immunity may succeed on the basis of some consideration additional to the confidentiality of the documents, as when the party claiming immunity is exercising a statutory function the effective performance of which would be impaired by disclosure: see, e.g. *Lonrho Ltd* v *Shell Petroleum* [1980] 1 WLR 627, HL. On the facts given, however, no such additional consideration is apparent.

**34.** An appropriately qualified expert may state his opinion on a matter calling for the expertise he has. The farmers are appropriately qualified: expertise may be acquired by experience as well as by study or paper qualifications, and both have been sheep farming in the locality for over 25 years. Their proposed evidence is clearly relevant to the issue as opposed to raising any collateral issue. Their proposed evidence is evidence of opinion, not fact, whether there is a risk of sheep contracting diseases if grazed on certain types of land, and this is a matter calling for expertise rather than a matter within the experience and knowledge of the judge as tribunal of fact. For all these reasons, [A] is correct and [B], [C] and [D] incorrect.

**35.** This question provides another factual scenario for application of the principles contained in s. 11 of the Civil Evidence Act 1968. [D] is the correct answer (and [A], [B] and [C] incorrect) for the reasons set out in the answer to Question 29, above.

**36.** The Civil Evidence Act 1968, s. 7(1) provides that:

'Subject to rules of Court, where in any civil proceedings a statement made by a person who is not called as a witness in those proceedings is given in evidence by virtue of section 2 of this Act . . . (b) evidence tending to prove that, whether before of after he made that statement, that person made . . . another statement inconsistent therewith shall be admissible for the purpose of showing that that person has contradicted himself . . .'

RSC Ord. 38, r. 31 provides that a party seeking to adduce evidence of an inconsistent statement under s. 7(1)(b) shall serve notice of his intention to adduce the evidence; and Ord. 38, r. 31(3) gives the Court a discretion to admit such evidence despite non-compliance with this notice of intention procedure.

**37.** [B] is correct because of the well-established rule of public policy that a witness in civil (or criminal) proceedings may not be asked to disclose the name of a police informer: see *R* v *Hardy* (1794) 24 State Tr 199. [A] is incorrect because confidentiality, *per se*, is not a sufficient ground of immunity from disclosure: see *Alfred Crompton Amusement Machines Ltd* v *Customs & Excise Commissioners (No. 2)* [1974] AC 405. [C] is incorrect because the only exception is in criminal cases in which enforcement of the rule would be likely to cause a miscarriage of justice: see *R* v *Hennessey* (1978) 68 Cr App R

419, CA, etc. [D] is incorrect because the judge is obliged to apply the rule even if the party entitled to its benefit does not invoke it: see per Lord Esher MR in *Marks* v *Beyfus* (1890) 25 QBD 494, CCA.

**38.** The Contempt of Court Act 1981, s. 10 provides that: 'No Court may require a person to disclose . . . the source of information contained in a publication for which he is responsible, unless it be established to the satisfaction of the Court that disclosure is necessary in the interests of justice or national security or for the prevention of disorder or crime'. It is a question of fact whether any given case comes within one of the four exceptions, and the burden of proving 'necessity' is on the party seeking disclosure: *Secretary of State for Defence* v *Guardian Newspapers Ltd* [1984] 3 All ER 601, HL.

**39.** The statement is admissible under s. 3 of the Criminal Procedure Act 1865, which applies to civil as well as criminal proceedings. It provides that a party producing a witness may, if the witness in the opinion of the judge proves 'adverse' (i.e. hostile), prove that he has made a statement inconsistent with his present testimony. Where such a statement is proved, it is clearly admissible to establish the witness's inconsistency. In civil proceedings, the statement is also admissible as evidence of any fact stated therein of which direct oral evidence by the witness would be admissible: Civil Evidence Act 1968, s. 3(1)(a).

**40.** The statements in [B], [C] and [D] are all accurate. [A] is incorrect because facts which are beyond serious dispute, sufficiently notorious or of common knowledge will be the subject of judicial notice *without* enquiry. The doctrine of judicial notice after enquiry is used in relation to facts which are neither notorious nor of common knowledge, which is why, under the doctrine, the judge may consult a variety of different sources before reaching a decision. See, e.g., *McQuaker* v *Goddard* [1940] 1 KB 687, CA, where the question being whether a camel was a wild or domestic animal, it was held that books about camels could be consulted and expert witnesses could give evidence concerning their behaviour, before the judge took judicial notice of the fact that they are domestic animals.

## CRIMINAL LITIGATION AND SENTENCING

**41**. [B], [C] and [D] indicate sentences which may lawfully be imposed. A sentence of detention in a young offender institution is available for an offender aged 15 and under 21 years of age whenever the offence is punishable with imprisonment in the case of an adult Criminal Justice Act 1982, s. 1A). The restriction on sentencing of young offenders to a term of 12 months in a young offender institution (to be increased to 2 years when the Criminal Justice and Public Order Act comes into force) applies only to those aged 15, 16 or 17 (Criminal Justice Act 1991, s. 1B and Powers of Criminal Courts Act 1973, s. 14). [A] indicates a sentence which cannot lawfully be imposed. A suspended sentence is a sentence of imprisonment which cannot be imposed on a person under 21 years of age (Powers of Criminal Courts Act 1973, s. 22).

**42**. Where the question of fitness to plead is raised, a jury should decide the issue (Criminal Procedure (Insanity) Act 1964, s. 4(5)). Hence [B] is correct. The flaw in the procedure was that the judge decided on the issue of fitness to plead. [A] is wrong. It is quite usual for the matter to be raised prior to arraignment in this way. [C] is wrong, since a hospital order is one of the orders specified as within the Court's powers in these circumstances (s. 5 of the 1964 Act). [D] is also wrong. Fitness to plead can be raised on a murder charge. The distinctive feature in such cases is that if the defendant is unfit to plead, but did commit the *actus reus* of the offence, the only disposition which the judge can make is an admission order to a hospital without limit of time.

**43**. Where the jury cannot agree, after all appropriate steps have been taken the judge will discharge them, The defendant is not acquitted, and may be re-tried if the prosecution so decide. In practice, it is usual for the prosecution to initiate a second trial. If the jury again fail to agree, the practice is for no evidence to be offered at the start of what would otherwise be the third trial.

[A] is therefore wrong, because it is up to the prosecution to decide and the word 'must' is incorrect. [B] is right. [C] is wrong since the prosecution require no leave to proceed to re-trial. [D] is also wrong, since the defendant has not been acquitted.

**44.** [A] and [C] are incorrect as the Court has no power to impose a custodial sentence and a probation order on the same occasion (*R* v *Mullervy* (1986) 8 Cr App R (S) 41 and *R* v *Duporte* (1989) 11 Cr App R (S) 116). [B] is incorrect and [D] is correct for it would be counsel's professional duty to draw the judge's attention to the mistake (*R* v *Komsta* (1990) *The Times*, 31 July, *R* v *Hartrey* (1993) 14 Cr App R (S) 507 and *R* v *Richards* (1993) *The Times*, 1 April). See also *R* v *Stuart* [1993] Crim LR 767, in which a wasted costs order was made against counsel for failing to have the case re-listed within 28 days under s. 47 of the Supreme Court Act 1981 in order that a sentencing error could be rectified.

**45.** The Court can amend an indictment before or at any stage of the trial, unless the amendment cannot be made without injustice (Indictments Act 1915, s. 5). [A] states the law correctly, and is the right choice. [B] is wrong because the counts in the indictment do not need to correspond with those found on committal, either at the start of the trial or thereafter. [C] is wrong because the indictment can be amended during trial, subject to the limits stated above. [D] is wrong since it is for the Court to amend the indictment.

**46.** This is a case where the guilty plea was entered under duress, and the rules relating to equivocal pleas apply (see *R* v *Huntingdon Crown Court ex parte Jordan* [1981] QB 857). [A] is wrong since the case will not be reheard in the Crown Court. It will be remitted to the magistrates for hearing on a not guilty plea, as stated in [B], which is the correct choice. [C] is wrong. The magistrates are no longer appraised of the matter and, in any event, the case would not be reheard in the Crown Court. [D] is also wrong, since it is the Crown Court rather than the magistrates which should determine that the case should be heard again by the magistrates.

**47.** In certain circumstances, the jury can bring in a verdict of guilty of an alternative offence. The general rule is contained in s. 6 of the Criminal Law Act 1967, which states that such a verdict can be returned where the alternative offence is contained, expressly or by implication, in the offence charged. (There are other statutory provisions relating to particular offences, none of which is relevant here.)

[A] is therefore correct. An allegation of robbery includes an allegation of theft, since robbery is theft with additional elements added. [B] is wrong. Theft *is* a less serious offence than robbery, but that is not the reason why the jury can return such a verdict. [C] is wrong because the deletion of particulars can be used to see whether an alternative verdict is *expressly* included in the charge. It does not, however, deal with the other possibility: that the alternative verdict is *impliedly* included in the charge, as it is here. [D] is wrong since alternative verdicts are available in the circumstances specified by s. 6 of the 1967 Act, inter alia.

**48.** Ian must serve an alibi notice in respect of the theft of the necklace. Such notice must be served at, or within 7 days of the end of, committal proceedings, if Ian is to be able to adduce 'evidence in support of an alibi' without the necessity of obtaining the judge's leave at his trial (Criminal Justice Act 1967, s. 11). 'Evidence in support of an alibi' encompasses evidence tending to show that, because he was in a particular place at a particular time, he was not in the place where the offence was committed. This is so even where the evidence will come from Ian himself (*Jackson* [1973] Crim LR 356).

But Ian need not serve notice of alibi in respect of the charge of living on the earnings of a prostitute. This is because the alibi provisions are applicable only where the offence alleged was committed at a particular place and time, as opposed to being committed in an unspecified geographical area over a lengthy period: *Hassan* [1970] 1 QB 423.

Hence [C] describes the law correctly, and the others are wrong.

**49.** [A] is correct and [B] incorrect as the maximum aggregate custodial sentence which the youth Court can impose for 2 or more indictable offences is 12 months, i.e. 6 months maximum per offence to run consecutively, provided that the aggregate term does not exceed 12 months' detention in a young offender institution. [C] and [D] are incorrect as the Crown Court has power to sentence the offender to a maximum of 12 months' detention in a young offender institution per offence, provided that the aggregate term does not exceed 12 months. (This will be increased to 2 years when the Criminal Justice and Public Order Act comes into force. See the Magistrates' Court Act 1980, s. 37 and the Powers of Criminal Courts Act 1973, s. 42.)

**50.** An accused whose submission of no case has been wrongly rejected has been deprived of the certainty (rather than the possibility) of an acquittal. The conviction should therefore be quashed, and option [A] is right (see *Abbott* [1955] 2 QB 497, *Juett* [1981] Crim LR 113, *Cockley* (1984) 79 Cr App R 181).

[B] is wrong, both because the accused is entitled to an acquittal, and because the case does not fit within the limited circumstances in which a *venire de novo* is possible (see *Rose* [1982] AC 822). [C] is wrong, because the accused would have been acquitted if the judge had ruled correctly. [D] is wrong, both for the reasons already canvassed, and because the Court of Appeal will avoid putting itself in the place of the jury.

**51.** The crucial point here is that the jury have retired. There is an absolute rule that, once the jury have been sent out to consider their verdict, no further evidence may be adduced: *Owen* [1952] 2 QB 362. The right answer, therefore, is [D].

As to [A], the jury can hear additional evidence for the prosecution if the judge gives leave, but only *before* they retire. [B] is excluded by *Owen*. [C] is wrong: the jury may ask questions after retirement.

**52**. An appeal against the refusal of bail by the magistrates may be heard by the Crown Court (Supreme Court Act 1981, s. 81), or the High Court (RSC Ord. 79, r. 9). The second judge should be informed of the first unsuccessful appeal. Hence [C] is right.

[A] is wrong, because no special leave is required for an application to the High Court. [B] is also wrong since an unsuccessful appeal to the High Court does not bar an application to the Crown Court. [D] is wrong in limiting the jurisdiction of the High Court to hear a bail application in this way.

**53**. Regarding [B], the Court when sentencing is entitled to take into account the prevalence of an offence in an area (*R* v *Cunningham* [1993] 1 WLR 183). Regarding [C], when considering seriousness, it is also entitled to take into account any previous convictions of the offender or any failure of his to respond to previous sentences (Criminal Justice Act 1991, s. 29(1)). The Court is also entitled to take into account the need to impose a sentence which is commensurate with the seriousness of the offence as stated in [D] – the 'just deserts' provision in s. 2(2)(a) of the Criminal Justice Act 1991. In *R* v *Cunningham*, Lord Taylor LCJ said that the phrase 'commensurate with the seriousness of the offence' in s. 2(2)(a) 'must mean commensurate with the punishment and deterrence which the seriousness of the offence requires'. He did, however, go on to say 'What section 2(2)(a) does prohibit is adding any extra length to the sentence which by those criteria is commensurate with the seriousness of the offence, simply to make an example of the defendant'. [A] is therefore the correct answer as an exemplary sentence would not be permissible.

**54**. By the Criminal Appeal Act 1968, s. 3, the Court of Appeal may in certain circumstances substitute for the verdict of the jury a verdict of guilty of an alternative offence. The power arises when (i) the jury could, on the indictment, have found the appellant guilty of the alternative offence, and (ii) it appears from the jury's verdict that they must have been satisfied of the facts proving the appellant guilty of the alternative offence.

Theft is an alternative verdict where burglary contrary to the Theft Act 1968, s. 9(1)(b) is charged. [C] is on the facts in this question the likeliest, course of action. [A] is unlikely, since it appears Daniel was guilty of theft, and the Court of Appeal has the power to substitute a conviction for theft. [B] would clearly be a wrong course to take, since Daniel is not guilty of burglary.

It is unlikely that the Court of Appeal will follow course [D]. The evidence for both prosecution and defence indicates that a re-trial will result in a verdict of guilty of theft (rather than not guilty, or guilty of burglary). A re-trial should be ordered only where the interests of justice so require (Criminal Appeal Act 1968, s. 7(1)).

**55.** Under the Magistrates' Courts Act 1980, s. 38, the magistrates have power to commit a triable either way offence to the Crown Court for sentence, provided that the offender is aged 18 or more, and they are of the opinion that greater punishment should be inflicted for the offence than they have power to impose. They are therefore empowered to commit the most serious of the offences under s. 38. As far as the other offences are concerned, they are able to commit these for sentence under s. 56 of the Criminal Justice Act 1967. This gives them power, when they are exercising powers under s. 38 of the 1980 Act, to commit for sentence in respect of any other offence (summary or indictable) which they have jurisdiction to deal with. It follows that [D] is correct, and all the others are wrong.

**56.** Whilst the judge is entitled to use a form of words to encourage the jury to reach a verdict, they nust not be subjected to any pressure. The case which lays down the form which such a direction ought to take is *Watson* [1988] QB 690. In sum, that case approves each of the formulae contained in [A], [B] and [C]. It also expressly rules out any reference by the judge to the unfortunate consequences of a failure to agree, such as cost and inconvenience (overruling *Walhein* (1952) 36 Cr App R 167). [D] therefore contains the direction which is forbidden, and it follows that [D] is the correct answer.

**57.** By proviso (i) of the Administration of Justice (Miscellaneous Provisions) Act 1933, s. 2(2)(a), an indictment may include 'either in substitution for or in addition to counts charging the offence for which he was committed, any counts [based on the evidence, including statements, at committal] . . . being counts which may lawfully be joined in the same indictment.' It follows that [A] is incorrect.

But the prosecution may not rely on this proviso to prefer an indictment consisting *entirely* of counts in respect of which there has been no committal for trial, even where the accused has been committed on other charges and the offences charged in the indictment are disclosed by the committal evidence (*Lombardi* [1989] 1 WLR 73). That is what has been done here, and it follows that the trial judge's decision was incorrect for the reason stated in [B].

[C] states the law too broadly in view of *Lombardi* and in the light of the words from the proviso quoted above: 'being counts which may lawfully be joined in the same indictment'. [D] is wrong, having no basis in law.


**58.** The correct answer is [A]. The relevant provision is the Criminal Justice Act 1991, sch. 2, para. 8(2)(b), which provides:

**8.**(1)  This paragraph applies where an offender in respect of whom a relevant order is in force —
    (a)  is convicted of an offence before the Crown Court .
. .

    (2)  If it appears to the Crown Court to be in the interests of justice to do so, having regard to circumstances which have arisen since the order was made, the Crown Court may
. . .

    (b)  revoke the order and deal with the offender, for the offence in respect of which the order was made, in any manner in which it could deal with him if he had just been convicted by or before the Court of the offence.

It was held in *R v Bennett* (1994) 15 Cr App R (S) 213 that the Crown Court had no power to revoke a probation order which was not still in force when the offender was sentenced for the later offence. The Crown Court may not therefore revoke the probation order and re-sentence the defendant in respect of the theft offence for which he was placed on probation in 1992, as the probation order is no longer in force. No action can be taken in respect of that theft offence.

**59.** The *Practice Direction (Crime: Sentence: Loss of Time)* [1980] 1 WLR 663 states that a direction for loss of time in the case of an unsucccessful application for leave to appeal 'will normally be made unless grounds are not only settled and signed by counsel, but also supported by the written opinion of counsel'. The terms of the direction therefore give a measure of protection from such a direction at the stage of application for leave. But no such protection is given where an application has been refused by the single judge, and is then renewed, whether or not counsel so advises. The applicant is vulnerable to a direction in these circumstances. [A] is therefore correct, [B] is wrong. It follows that [C] and [D] are also wrong.

**60.** The sentence is wrong in law since a defendant cannot be sentenced to a term of imprisonment before the age of 21. The Criminal Appeal Act 1968, s. 11 provides that no appeal shall lie against sentence unless either:

(a)   the appellant has been granted leave to appeal by the Court of Appeal; or

(b)   the trial judge certifies that the case is fit for appeal against sentence.

[A] is therefore wrong. Arnold *does* need leave to appeal, since his appeal is against sentence. [B] states the law correctly. [C] is wrong because the Registrar has no power to grant leave, [D] is incorrect – the trial judge is given this power by s. 11 of the 1968 Act.

## CRIMINAL EVIDENCE

**61.**   [B] is correct (and [A] incorrect) because the statement is in a document; the statement contains facts of which direct oral evidence would be admissible; the document was created by David in the course of his occupation; and the information contained in the document was supplied to him by a person, himself, who had personal knowledge of the matters dealt with (s. 24(1)). If the statement was prepared for the purposes of a criminal investigation, then it would be necessary to satisfy the requirements of s. 24(4): on the facts given, the requirement in s. 24(4)(iii) would be satisfied (maker cannot be expected to have any recollection). The statement is only admissible 'in principle' because of the discretion to exclude under s. 25 of the 1988 Act. [C] is incorrect because there is nothing to satisfy the requirements of one of the paragraphs of s. 23(2) or the requirements of s. 23(3). [D] is incorrect because there is nothing on the facts to suggest that the statement is admissible for some relevant purpose other than the truth of its contents.

**62.** The out-of-Court statement allegedly made by Amanda is admissible hearsay: it is a confession as defined in the Police and Criminal Evidence Act 1984, s. 82(1) ('any statement . . . adverse to the person who made it') and admissible under s. 76(1) of that Act. Concerning a voir dire, where the prosecution intend to rely on an oral confession and the defence case is simply that the accused never made it, no question of admissibility arises for the judge to decide and there is therefore no need for a voir dire; the only issue is a question of fact, whether or not the accused made the confession, and that is for the jury: see *Ajodha* v *The State* [1951] 2 All ER 193, PC, applied in *R* v *Flemming* (1988) 86 Cr App R 32, CA. It would be otherwise, of course, had Amanda alleged oppression, something said or done likely to render unreliable any consequent confession, or some impropriety (apart from the alleged invention of the confession).

**63.** [D] is correct (and [A] incorrect) because the statement was made in a document; the statement contains facts of which direct oral evidence would be admissible; and the person who made it is dead (Criminal Justice Act 1988, s. 23(1) and (2)(a)). Subject to the discretion to exclude under s. 25 of that Act, it is therefore admissible hearsay. [B] is incorrect because the document was not created or received by a person in the course of a trade, business, profession etc. (s. 24(1)(i)). [C] is incorrect because a dying declaration is admissible only if, inter alia, (i) it relates to the cause of the victim's injuries and (ii) at the time when it was made, the victim was under a settled hopeless expectation of death.

**64.** [A] is correct (and [C] incorrect) because of the decision in *DPP* v *Marshall* [1988] 3 All ER 683, DC, where on a charge of selling intoxicating liquor without a licence, it was held that evidence of purchases by plain clothes officers was admissible. [B] is incorrect because of the very wording of s. 78 of the Police and Criminal Evidence Act 1984: 'if it appears to the Court that, having regard to all the circumstances, including the circumstances in which the evidence was obtained . . .'. Concerning [D], see *R* v *Christou* [1992] QB 979, CA. In that case, it was held that Code C (which includes the requirement to caution) is intended to protect suspects who are, or may believe themselves to be, vulnerable to abuse or pressure from officers acting as such. Although it was also held that it would be wrong for the police to adopt an undercover pose to enable them to ask questions about an offence uninhibited by the Code and with the effect of circumventing it (in which case, a judge could exclude under s. 78), on the facts the officers' questions were not about the offence but, for the most part, simply necessary to maintain their cover. *Cf R* v *Bryce* [1992] 4 All ER 567, CA.

**65.** [A] is incorrect because the conditions of admissibility contained in s. 76 apply to a 'confession' and this is defined to include 'any statement . . . whether made to a person in authority or not' (s. 82(1) of the 1984 Act). [B] is incorrect because under s. 76(2)(b) the judge may only rule a confession admissible if, 'notwithstanding that it may be true', he is satisfied beyond reasonable doubt that it was not obtained in consequence of anything done or said etc. [C] is correct: s. 76(2)(b) requires a causal connection between what was said or done and the confession. Thus if the judge was satisfied that the confession was not obtained 'in consequence of Beatrice's statement', this could have been the justification for his decision to admit it. There is no authority to support [D].

**66.** [B] is correct because where, at a trial on indictment, the case against the accused depends wholly or substantially on a confession by him and the Court is satisfied that (i) he is mentally handicapped and (ii) the confession was not made in the presence of an independent person, the Court shall warn the jury that there is a special need for caution: see the Police and Criminal Evidence Act 1984, s. 77. There is no authority to support [A]. [C] is incorrect: there is no common-law or statutory authority to permit a mentally-handicapped person to give his or her evidence *unsworn*. [D] is incorrect because the proper test of the competence of a mentally-handicapped person is not whether he or she understands the divine sanction of the oath, but the secular test adopted (in the case of children) in *R v Hayes* [1977] 1 WLR 234: see *R v Bellamy* (1985) 82 Cr App R 222, CA.

**67.** [D] is correct (and [A] and [C] incorrect) because of the ruling of the Court of Appeal in *R v Cook* [1987] 1 All ER 1049, that photofits, together with sketches and photographs, are in a class of their own to which neither the rule against hearsay nor the rule against previous consistent statements is applicable. On the particular facts, see also *R v Dodson; R v Williams* (1984) 79 Cr App R 220, CA, where it was held that photographs taken by security cameras installed at a building society office at which an armed robbery was attempted, were admissible, being relevant to the issues of whether an offence was committed and, if so, who committed it. [B] is incorrect because although a document, for the purposes of the Criminal Justice Act 1988, s. 24, is defined to include a photograph (sch. 2, para. 5 of the 1988 Act), it is difficult to see, inter alia, how the information contained in the photograph could sensibly be said to have been 'supplied by a person . . . who had . . . personal knowledge of the matters dealt with'.

**68.** [B] is correct because the statement was made in a document; the statement contains facts of which direct oral evidence would be admissible; and its maker is dead (Criminal Justice Act 1988, s. 23(1) and (2)(a)). [A] is incorrect because the Police and Criminal Evidence Act 1984, s. 76, which governs the admissibility of confessions in criminal cases, only admits 'a confession made by an accused person'

(s. 76(1)). [C] is incorrect because the statement was clearly not made in circumstances of such spontaneity or involvement in the event, i.e. the murder, that the possibility of concoction can be disregarded: see *Ratten* v *R* [1972] AC 378, PC etc. [D] is incorrect because a dying declaration is admissible at a trial for murder or manslaughter only if, inter alia, it was made by the victim and relates to the cause of his or her injuries.

**69.** [B] is correct because the statement is admissible original evidence, i.e. evidence tendered for a relevant purpose other than proving the truth of the facts it contains, namely to show what Robin, who heard it, thought or believed, which has an obvious relevance to his defence: *cf Subramaniam* v *Public Prosecutor* [1956] 1 WLR 965. [A] is incorrect because the event in question, the purchase of a video, can hardly be said to have been so unusual, startling or dramatic as to have dominated the thoughts of the colleague and given him or her no real opportunity for reasoned reflection: see per Lord Ackner in *R* v *Andrews* [1957] 1 All ER 513, HL, at pp. 520–1. [C] is incorrect because the statement, if tendered for the truth of its contents, will be inadmissible hearsay. [D] is incorrect because the Criminal Justice Act 1988, s. 23, only admits statements made by a person 'in a document'.

**70.** In *R* v *Goodway* [1993] 4 All ER 894, CA, it was held that a *Lucas* direction should be given, save where it is otiose, whenever lies are or may be relied on in support of prosecution evidence of the accused's guilt, and not merely in corroboration and identification cases. In *R* v *Lucas* [1981] QB 720, it was held that to be capable of amounting to corroboration (i) the lie must be deliberate (ii) it must relate to a material issue (iii) the motive for it must be a realisation of guilt and a fear of the truth and (iv) it must clearly be shown to be a lie by admission or by evidence from an independent witness, i.e. a witness other than the witness requiring corroboration or a warning. There is no requirement that the lie should be in writing or otherwise recorded in documentary form.

**71.** (1) is incorrect because a confession may be excluded under the Police and Criminal Evidence Act 1984, s. 76(2)(b) where there is not even a suspicion of impropriety: see per Lord Lane CJ in *R v Fulling* [1987] 2 All ER 65, CA and, e.g., *R v Harvey* [1988] Crim LR 241, CC. (2) is correct because the test of reliability under s. 76(2)(b) is hypothetical, in the sense that on its very wording it applies to 'any confession' which might be made by the accused: see *R v Barry* (1991) 95 Cr App R 384, CA.

**72.** (1) is incorrect, because under the Police and Criminal Evidence Act 1984, s. 76(2), the defence may raise the question of admissibility merely by making a 'representation' to the Court that the confession was or may have been obtained by the methods described – the holding of a voir dire is thus not conditional upon evidence in support of such a representation. (2) is incorrect because under s. 76(2), a confession obtained by oppression will be excluded 'notwithstanding that it may be true'.

**73.** [C] is correct (and [A] incorrect) because the statement is in a document; the statement contains facts of which direct oral evidence would be admissible; the document was created by Luke in the course of his occupation; the information contained in the document was supplied to him by Jim, who had personal knowledge of the matters dealt with; and the statement having been prepared for the purposes of a criminal investigation, Jim is dead (s. 24(1) and (4)). The statement is only admissible 'in principle' because of the requirement of leave under s. 26 and the discretion to exclude under s. 25. [B] is incorrect because s. 23 applies only to first-hand documentary hearsay. In other words, although direct oral evidence of the facts by Jim would be admissible, he has not 'made a statement in a document' – he did not read and sign the document nor check that what Luke had written down was an accurate record of what he had said: *R v McGillivray* (1993) 97 Cr App R 232, CA. [D] is incorrect because, among other reasons, under that common-law exception to the hearsay rule, the declaration must relate to an act performed by the deceased, and not by another or others: *The Henry Coxon* (1878) 3 PD 156.

**74.** [A] is correct because the out-of-Court statement is being tendered for the truth of its contents but is not covered by any exception to the rule against hearsay. [B] is incorrect because s. 23 applies only to first-hand documentary hearsay: see the answer to Question 73, above. [C] is incorrect because the information contained in the document created by Luke was supplied indirectly, but the person through whom it was supplied, Ken, did not receive it in the course of a trade, business, profession etc. (s. 24(2)). [D] is incorrect because, among other reasons, under that common-law exception to the hearsay rule, the record must be compiled by a person acting under a public duty to record findings so that the public may refer to them: see, e.g., *Lilley* v *Pettit* [1946] KB 401, DC.


**75.** [C] is correct (and [A] and [B] incorrect) because in *R* v *Turnbull* [1977] QB 224, Lord Widgery CJ held that whenever the case against an accused depends wholly or substantially on the correctness of one or more identifications of the accused, which the defence allege to be mistaken, and in the judgment of the judge the quality of the identifying evidence is poor, he or she should direct an acquittal unless there is other evidence, which need not be corroboration in the strict sense, which goes to support the correctness of the identification. As to [D], a judge should not direct a jury that he would have withdrawn the case from them had he thought that there was insufficient identification evidence, because the jury may thereby mistakenly conclude that the evidence is sufficiently strong for them to convict: *R* v *Smith and Doe* (1986) 85 Cr App R 197, CA.


**76.** [A] is correct (and [C] and [D] incorrect) because if a man admits something of which he knows nothing, it is of no real evidential value: see *Comptroller of Customs* v *Western Electric Co. Ltd* [1966] AC 367, PC, where an admission as to the country of origin of imported goods, made in reliance on marks and labels borne by the goods, was held to be evidentially worthless. The suggestion in [B] that the admissions may be admissible not for the truth of their contents, but as original evidence, i.e. simply to show that the statements were made, is incorrect: an out-of-Court statement is only admissible as original evidence if it serves some relevant purpose other than that of proving the truth of the facts it contains but, on the facts given, there is no such relevant purpose.

**77.** In criminal proceedings, it seems that a witness cannot claim privilege in respect of questions the answers to which tend to incriminate his or her spouse: see per Lord Diplock in *Rio Tinto Zinc Corporation* v *Westinghouse Electric Corporation* [1978] AC 547 at p. 637. However, even if such a privilege does exist, it could not be claimed on the facts given because the evidence against the spouse is already sufficiently strong for her to have been charged with the importation of the cocaine, and her trial will take place whether or not Dick answers the question: *Rio Tinto Zinc Corporation* v *Westinghouse Electric Corporation*, ibid.

**78.** [D] is correct (and [A], [B] and [C] incorrect) because where the jury can form their own opinion about a particular matter without the assistance of an expert, that matter being within their own knowledge and experience, expert opinion evidence is inadmissible because unnecessary: per Lawton LJ in *R* v *Turner* [1975] QB 834 at p. 841. Thus expert psychiatric evidence is generally inadmissible on the question of *mens rea*, credibility, provocation or the reliability of a confession (although it is a practical necessity in order to establish insanity or diminished responsibility, and will be admissible on the question of *mens rea* or the reliability of a confession if the accused comes into the class of mental defective). Compare the facts with those of *R* v *Turner*, ibid.

**79.** [B] is correct (and [C] and [D] are incorrect) because under the Police and Criminal Evidence Act 1984, s. 67(9), the Codes apply not only to police officers, but also to other persons 'charged with the duty of investigating offences or charging offenders'; and whether a person satisfies this test is a question of fact in each case: per Watkins LJ in *R* v *Seelig* [1991] 4 All ER 429, CA, at p. 439. As to [A], Naomi's questioning did amount to an interview, which is defined as the questioning of a person regarding his involvement or suspected involvement in a criminal offence: Note 11A, Code C.

**80.** [C] is correct because the only relevant purpose of tendering the statement of the eye-witness would be to prove the truth of the facts it contains (that the man who threw the brick had run into the building on the other side of the square) and it is therefore inadmissible hearsay: cf *R* v *Gibson* (1887) 18 QBD 537. [A] is incorrect because although at common law there is a *res gestae* exception to the hearsay rule in the case of contemporaneous statements explaining an act, the statement must be made by the person who performed the act: *Howe* v *Malkin* (1878) 40 LT 196. [B] is incorrect because inadmissible hearsay remains inadmissible even if it can be categorised as circumstantial evidence. The reason given in [D] is incorrect because the statement of the eye-witness is clearly relevant to the identification of the criminal.

# APPENDIX 5

## CIVIL LITIGATION SYLLABUS FOR MCT- PART 1

High Court and County Court jurisdiction.

Computation of time and non-compliance with Rules of Court.

Commencement in the County Court including types of proceedings.

Commencement in the High Court, including writ and originating summons procedure, service and pleadings.

Parties, joinder, representative actions, consolidation of actions, intervening.

Service outside the jurisdiction with and without leave. Third Party procedure and contribution notices.

Procedure on interlocutory applications.

Default judgments in the High Court and County Court, including judgment in default of pleading.

Summary judgment in the High Court and County Court, interim payments and summary possession proceedings.

Interlocutory injunctions, *Mareva* injunctions and *Anton Piller* orders.

Discovery and inspection of documents.

*Norwich Pharmacal* orders; pre-action discovery under SCA 1981, s. 33(2); discovery against non-parties under SCA 1981, s. 34(2); orders for the inspection of property including orders under SCA 1981, s. 34(3) and SCA 1981, s. 33(1); interim delivery up of goods.

Directions, including automatic directions.

Interrogatories.

# EVIDENCE SYLLABUS FOR MCT–PART 1

Facts open to proof or disproof. Formal Admissions. Basic concepts: relevance, admissibility, weight and sufficiency.
Varieties of evidence.
Discretion.
Functions of Judge and Jury.
Burden and Standard of proof.
Presumptions including conflicting presumptions.
Witnesses: attendance of witnesses and procedural issues, sworn and unsworn evidence and competence and compellability.
Examination-in-chief including leading questions, refreshing memory, previous consistent statements and unfavourable and hostile witnesses.
Cross-examination including liability to cross-examination, cross-examination on documents, cross-examination as to credit, the character of the complainant on charges of rape, previous inconsistent statements, and the rule of finality of answers to collateral questions and exceptions thereto.
Re-examination.
Similar fact evidence.
Character evidence including the Criminal Evidence Act 1898, s. 1, and the right to silence in Court.

# CRIMINAL LITIGATION SYLLABUS FOR MCT–PART 1

*Preliminary Matters*

Police powers of arrest; detention at a police station under the Police and Criminal Evidence Act regime; access to legal advice; Codes of Practice issued under PACE 1984; 'serious arrestable offences'; charges; issue of process at a Magistrates' Court; legal aid; costs orders.

*Remands and Bail*

Difference between simple adjournment and a remand; situations where a remand must be used; duration of remands; general right to bail; attaching conditions to release on bail; sureties and forfeiture; applying for bail; limit on number of applications; appeals to or variations by a judge (of the High Court or Crown Court); custody time limits.

*Preliminary Appearances*

Classification of offences; determination of mode of trial; special provisions for criminal damage; advance disclosure of information; Criminal Justice Act 1988, ss. 40 and 41.

*Summary Trial*

Trial of a charge or summons; joint trial of separate informations; proceeding in the accused's absence; guilty pleas by post; committals for sentence to the Crown Court (under the Magistrates' Courts Act 1980, ss. 37 and 38); appeals to the Crown Court; applications to the Divisional Court for judicial review or appeals by way of case stated.

*Juveniles and the Courts*

Who is a juvenile; the work of the Youth Court; which Courts can try juveniles; which Courts can pass sentence on juveniles; limits on sentencing powers; committals for trial or sentence; publicity and public access; use of cautions by police.

# APPENDIX 6

## CIVIL LITIGATION SYLLABUS FOR MCT-PART 2

The subjects listed under Civil Litigation for MCT – PART 1 (see Appendix 5) *AND* in addition to those subjects, the following:

Amendment of process and pleadings; misjoinder.
Limitation including amendment after the expiry of a limitation period.
Renewal of process.
Dismissal for want of prosecution, striking out, stays and discontinuance.
Security for costs, provisional damages.
Payment In and withdrawing payments in.
Notices to admit and produce.
Setting down for trial.
Hearsay admissible in civil proceedings.
Exchange of witnesses' statements.
Experts, including obtaining facilities for examination, directions, exchange of reports, procedure at trial.
Preliminary issues, witnesses and subpoenas, trial procedure.
Costs and Legal Aid.
Drawing up judgments; consent orders; *Tomlin* orders (in outline only).
Enforcement (in outline only).
Interpleader.
References to the European Court.
Appeals (in outline only).

# EVIDENCE SYLLABUS FOR MCT–PART 2

The subjects listed under Evidence for MCT – PART 1 (see Appendix 5) *AND* in addition to those subjects, the following:

The hearsay rule including its scope, original evidence, implied assertions, negative hearsay and statements produced by calculators etc.

Statutory and common-law exceptions to the hearsay rule including the relevant Rules of Supreme Court.

Confessions including all relevant sections of the Police and Criminal Evidence Act 1984 and the Codes of Practice.

Illegally and improperly obtained evidence.

Opinion evidence including the relevant Rules of Supreme Court and Crown Court Rules.

Judgments as evidence of the facts on which they are based including exceptions to the rule in *Hollington* v *Hewthorn*, convictions of the accused and convictions of persons other than the accused.

Corroboration.

Identification.

Privilege including privacy and confidential relationships.

Public interest immunity.

Judicial Notice.

Estoppel as a rule of evidence.

Documentary evidence.

Real evidence.


# CRIMINAL LITIGATION AND SENTENCING SYLLABUS FOR MCT–PART 2

The subjects listed under Criminal Litigation for MCT – PART 1 (see Appendix 5) *AND* in addition to those subjects, the following:

*Committal Proceedings*

Types of committal hearing under the Magistrates' Courts Act 1980, s. 61(1) and (2); Attorney-General's guidelines in identification cases; procedure at a committal hearing; submission of no case to answer; legal effect of a discharge; 'second-chance' committal proceedings; witness orders for Crown

Court; alibi warnings; voluntary bills of indictment; notices of transfer.

## Indictments, Pleas and Crown Court Preliminaries

Prosecution duty of disclosure; the structure of an indictment; separate counts and duplicity; joining several counts and accused in one indictment; amending indictments; use of alternative counts; pleas by the accused; fitness to plead; change of plea; plea to an alternative offence; abuse of process.

## Jury Trials

The sequence of a jury trial; absence of accused from Court; when opening or closing speeches may be made; seeing the judge in his room about plea or sentence; empanelling a jury; procedure where admissibility of evidence is disputed; making a formal admission; submission of no case to answer; alibi evidence; expert evidence; functions of judge and jury; contents of a summing-up; directions to a jury after their retirement; discharge of jurors; the verdict of the jury; majority verdicts; verdict of guilty of an alternative offence.

## Appeals to the Court of Appeal

Certificate from the trial judge; getting leave to appeal from a single judge of the Court of Appeal; appeals as of right; grounds of appeal against conviction – Criminal Appeal Act 1968, s. 2; appeal against sentence; appeals on fresh evidence; powers of the single judge; powers of the Court of Appeal; directions for loss of time.

## Sentencing

Basic sentencing powers of the Magistrates' and Crown Courts; sentencing procedure in both the Magistrates' and Crown Court; maximum and minimum for common types of sentence or order; when such sentences or orders can be used.

# ANSWER SHEET

Read the instructions before you start to fill in the answers.

## INSTRUCTIONS

1. Use the HB pencil provided.
2. Fill in the boxes like this ▬ not like this ✗ ✓
3. Fill in the boxes to indicate the subjects and whether this is a resit.
4. Write in your candidate number and the examination date in the spaces provided **and** fill in the boxes below.
5. Write your name and signature in the spaces provided.
6. Each question has four possible answers lettered A to D. Read all four answers **in full** before making a selection. Select the answer which you think is correct/best and indicate it on the answer sheet by filling in the appropriate box.
7. If you fill in 2 or more boxes in any question, that question will carry no mark.
8. Erase all mistakes thoroughly using the eraser provided.

## SUBJECT

Evidence & Civil Litigation [ ]

Evidence & Criminal Litigation [ ]

Is this a resit?  Yes [ ]   No [ ]

## CANDIDATE NUMBER

[0] [0] [0]
[1] [1] [1]
[2] [2] [2]
[3] [3] [3]
[4] [4] [4]
[5] [5] [5]
[6] [6] [6]
[7] [7] [7]
[8] [8] [8]
[9] [9] [9]

## DATE OF EXAM
### DAY  MONTH  YEAR

DAY:
[0] [1] [2] [3]

MONTH:
[0] [0]
[1] [1]
[2]
[3]
[4]
[5]
[6]
[7]
[8]
[9]

YEAR:
[0] [0]
[1] [1]
[2] [2]
[3] [3]
[4] [4]
[5] [5]
[6] [6]
[7] [7]
[8] [8]
[9] [9]

| | | | | |
|---|---|---|---|---|
| 1 | [A] [B] [C] [D] | 21 | [A] [B] [C] [D] | 41 | [A] [B] [C] [D] | 61 | [A] [B] [C] [D] |
| 2 | [A] [B] [C] [D] | 22 | [A] [B] [C] [D] | 42 | [A] [B] [C] [D] | 62 | [A] [B] [C] [D] |
| 3 | [A] [B] [C] [D] | 23 | [A] [B] [C] [D] | 43 | [A] [B] [C] [D] | 63 | [A] [B] [C] [D] |
| 4 | [A] [B] [C] [D] | 24 | [A] [B] [C] [D] | 44 | [A] [B] [C] [D] | 64 | [A] [B] [C] [D] |
| 5 | [A] [B] [C] [D] | 25 | [A] [B] [C] [D] | 45 | [A] [B] [C] [D] | 65 | [A] [B] [C] [D] |

| 6 | [A] [B] [C] [D] | 26 | [A] [B] [C] [D] | 46 | [A] [B] [C] [D] | 66 | [A] [B] [C] [D] |
|---|---|---|---|---|
| 7 | [A] [B] [C] [D] | 27 | [A] [B] [C] [D] | 47 | [A] [B] [C] [D] | 67 | [A] [B] [C] [D] |
| 8 | [A] [B] [C] [D] | 28 | [A] [B] [C] [D] | 48 | [A] [B] [C] [D] | 68 | [A] [B] [C] [D] |
| 9 | [A] [B] [C] [D] | 29 | [A] [B] [C] [D] | 49 | [A] [B] [C] [D] | 69 | [A] [B] [C] [D] |
| 10 | [A] [B] [C] [D] | 30 | [A] [B] [C] [D] | 50 | [A] [B] [C] [D] | 70 | [A] [B] [C] [D] |

| 11 | [A] [B] [C] [D] | 31 | [A] [B] [C] [D] | 51 | [A] [B] [C] [D] | 71 | [A] [B] [C] [D] |
|---|---|---|---|---|
| 12 | [A] [B] [C] [D] | 32 | [A] [B] [C] [D] | 52 | [A] [B] [C] [D] | 72 | [A] [B] [C] [D] |
| 13 | [A] [B] [C] [D] | 33 | [A] [B] [C] [D] | 53 | [A] [B] [C] [D] | 73 | [A] [B] [C] [D] |
| 14 | [A] [B] [C] [D] | 34 | [A] [B] [C] [D] | 54 | [A] [B] [C] [D] | 74 | [A] [B] [C] [D] |
| 15 | [A] [B] [C] [D] | 35 | [A] [B] [C] [D] | 55 | [A] [B] [C] [D] | 75 | [A] [B] [C] [D] |

| 16 | [A] [B] [C] [D] | 36 | [A] [B] [C] [D] | 56 | [A] [B] [C] [D] | 76 | [A] [B] [C] [D] |
|---|---|---|---|---|
| 17 | [A] [B] [C] [D] | 37 | [A] [B] [C] [D] | 57 | [A] [B] [C] [D] | 77 | [A] [B] [C] [D] |
| 18 | [A] [B] [C] [D] | 38 | [A] [B] [C] [D] | 58 | [A] [B] [C] [D] | 78 | [A] [B] [C] [D] |
| 19 | [A] [B] [C] [D] | 39 | [A] [B] [C] [D] | 59 | [A] [B] [C] [D] | 79 | [A] [B] [C] [D] |
| 20 | [A] [B] [C] [D] | 40 | [A] [B] [C] [D] | 60 | [A] [B] [C] [D] | 80 | [A] [B] [C] [D] |

# Srid

GW00706009

JULIA HOLT & SHUBHRA PHALKE

Sridevi was a child star
at four years old.
Now she is the Queen Bee of Bollywood.
She has been the top Indian film heroine
for more than ten years.

People pay to see her in a film
and it doesn't matter who the other actors are.
Some actors don't like this
because they want to be stars as well.

She is such a big star
that some people in the film industry
are too scared to talk to her.
Sridevi is like Amitabh Bachchan.
She takes any part in her stride.

The Queen Bee
has played two parts in the same film.
She played a love sick girl and the girl's mother
in the film *Lamhe*.

Amitabh Bachchan asked Sridevi
to come to England with him in 1990.
They did a show at Wembley
and she came in riding on an elephant's back.
She was dressed as the snake woman
from her famous film *Nagina*.

The two big superstars
have also acted together
in films like *Khuda Gawah*.
In this film Sridevi again played two parts,
both mother and daughter.
She enjoyed playing the older woman best.

*Sridevi – known for playing cheerful, bubbly people.* ▶

Sridevi admits
that she still has a lot to learn about acting.
"For an actress there can be no beginning
and no end," she says,
"She has to keep going,
taking on new parts."

In films she usually plays cheerful, bubbly people.
But she says
"I am not like this in real life,
I am a quiet person.
Acting and real life are so different."

In the film *Sadma*
she played a woman
who has the voice and mind
of a six year-old girl.
Sridevi did this without special training.
She is famous for her baby voice.

Her mother Rajeswari takes good care of her.
She worries that Sridevi has not grown up
and is still a child at heart.

Sridevi lives with all her family around her.
For ten years
she lived in Bombay hotels,
paid for by the film industry.

But now she lives
in an apartment in Bombay.
She doesn't like to be alone
 but she does enjoy cooking
and watching films on her video.

Sridevi is called 'thunder thighs' in the magazines.
Her mother Rajeswari makes sure
she doesn't eat too many sweets.
Rajeswari was the person who said
that the four year old Sridevi
was going to be a star one day.

Now she is in her late twenties
and her mother still looks after the star's life.
She says "My mother is my best friend."

This does not mean
that she wants to stay single.
Magazines are always linking
her to the men in her films.

She has no plans to marry at the moment.
She says her perfect man
"must be simple, he must not be talkative.
I would like a tall man
so I can wear my high heels."

She is not the most beautiful actress
in Indian films today,
but she does have a natural acting ability.
People have said she has a classical beauty,
with pale skin, large eyes,
a rosebud mouth and a full figure.

◀ *Now in her late twenties but still happier with her family around her.*

One of Sridevi's talents
is her ability to pick up dance steps very quickly.
She has had no dance training but she says
"I have a God-given talent for dance."
In one of her latest films
*Roop Ki Rani Choron Ka Raja*
she shows her dancing talents at their best.
But when she worked with Sunjay Dutt
on the film *Gumraah,*
she said he was an even better dancer than her.

She feels very lucky to have the talents that she has.
Acting in films is very easy for her.
As she says
"I have never had to struggle for anything in my
life."
To her, working in films is a job,
like going to the office.

*A western look for Sridevi, she does not enjoy travelling* ▶
*and would always rather be at home.*

The only thing she doesn't like is travelling.
She has already lost one part in a Hollywood film
because she didn't want to be in the USA for too
long.

People say of her that she is overweight,
overpaid and over the top.
But the Queen Bee of Bollywood still makes money.